THE FOURTH OF JULY

PROFILES IN HISTORY

....

THE FOURTH OF JULY
AND THE FOUNDING OF AMERICA

PETER DE BOLLA

PROFILE BOOKS

First published in Great Britain in 2007 by
Profile Books Ltd
3A Exmouth House
Pine Street
Exmouth Market
London EC1R 0JH
www.profilebooks.com

1 3 5 7 9 10 8 6 4 2

Typeset in Palatino by MacGuru Ltd
info@macguru.org.uk
Printed and bound in Great Britain by
Clays, Bungay, Suffolk

A CIP catalogue record for this book is available from the British Library.

ISBN 978 1 86197 850 9

The paper this book is printed on is certified by the © 1996 Forest Stewardship
Council A.C. (FSC). It is ancient-forest friendly. The printer holds FSC chain of
custody SGS-COC-2061

FSC

Mixed Sources

Product group from well-managed
forests and other controlled sources

Cert no. SGS-COC-2061
www.fsc.org
© 1996 Forest Stewardship Council

CONTENTS

1. *The Assembly Room in the State House, Philadelphia, painted by John Trumbull between 1785, when he began studies for the image, and 1818 when it was completed.*

INTRODUCTION

If there is any one thing that has singularly determined the shape and focus for the story of the Fourth of July it is this image. It depicts a moment which in many of the narratives recounting the creation of the United States of America is said to be *the* originative moment. There are other moments, for sure, which might make a similar claim: the resolution of Congress to adopt the Constitution, for example. But none has been represented in so varied media or contributed so significantly to the iconology of the United States. The painting itself has three versions and it has been reproduced at various times on postage stamps, currency and china, not to mention the hundreds of thousands of prints and photographs which have been taken from it. It is easy to understand why its dissemination has been so extensive since it documents the birthday of the nation. It is a snapshot of what transpired on 4 July 1776. Literally millions of people have seen this version of the painting which hangs in the Rotunda of the Capitol in Washington, DC. It was commissioned by Congress in a vote of 6 February 1817 authorising the fourth president, James Madison, to approach the artist John Trumbull with a request that he create four paintings commemorating the history of American independence. The title of the painting is *The Declaration of Independence* (for full image, see the endpapers).

Many of the men depicted, life size, seated around the edges of the room are no longer prominent characters in the common knowledge of contemporary Americans, notwithstanding the voluminous literature, both scholarly and popular, on the founding of the nation. Some of them, even in their own lifetimes, were perhaps never particularly well known outside the colony or even town in which they lived. But collectively they are notorious. This is the body of men who comprised the Second Continental Congress: these are the signatories to the Declaration of Independence. Each of them (excepting the man with the hat, the only man wearing a hat, standing in front of the door on the left-hand side), painstakingly rendered in portrait likeness by the artist, assented to the irrevocable step of signalling to the world at large the separation of the colonies from the mother country, thereby instituting the process that was to lead to the creation of the first modern republic: the United States of America. In so far as any snapshot can encapsulate a process this image conveys the signal moment in the story of the Fourth of July.

Although the events of that day in 1776 have been celebrated, for the most part continuously, since 1777, accounts have varied of what precisely *did* occur in the State House in Philadelphia when these men collectively agreed to the wording of a document that had been drafted primarily by one man, the tall figure in the central group of the painting standing closest to the left side of the desk with a document in his hands, the man who would become the third president of the republic, Thomas Jefferson. Over the course of the following chapters the extent of this variation will become clear. But I shall begin with our own moment in time, with what one might reasonably expect most people today to know about 4 July 1776.

The land mass we now refer to as North America was, in 1776, home to thirteen colonies, all of them independently founded at different times over the previous 169 years and each administered by separate internal institutions. Each was beholden to the British government under the provisions of its own distinct charter and legal instruments which collectively determined that relationship as colonial. By the middle of the eighteenth century those relations had become very strained and by the time of the Stamp Act in 1765, which levied a tax on documents, newspapers and nearly every form of paper used in the colonies, many citizens were beginning to advocate independence from the mother country.

Although each of the colonies administered its own affairs it had become clear by 1765 that acting in concert over the Stamp Act would be advantageous. In October of that year thirty-seven delegates representing each of the colonies met in New York to draw up a plan of action. Ten years later, by the time the Second Continental Congress first met in May 1775, irritation and dissatisfaction with King George III's behaviour towards the colonies was running at such a pace that the political will to launch a revolution was in the ascendant. His Majesty's attempts to steer a course away from confrontation were less than half-hearted: as far as many of his ministers were concerned the hotheads in the colonies were 'rebels' and needed to be brought back into line by military force. When the shot heard around the world was fired in April 1775 both sides began to be drawn into a confrontation which was unlikely to end amicably. And so by the summer of 1776 'independency', as it was referred to at the time, was seen by many as the inevitable next step. This is where the story of the Fourth of July begins.

Of the many and varied events that might be 'common knowledge' about that day in 1776, what appears to be undisputed is that something momentous occurred in the State House in Philadelphia. Here, in words taken from a book entitled *The Declaration of Independence* by Hal Marcovitz, one of a series for young students called 'American Symbols and their Meanings', is how that story is told:

> [O]n July 4 the Congress intended to vote specifically on the declaration drafted by Jefferson …
>
> The delegates entered the Philadelphia State House through the large doorway facing Chestnut Street. Above the door hung the royal *coat of arms* – the final reminder to them that they were still living under the oppressive will of the King of England.
>
> The delegates met in the white-paneled meeting room on the east side of the building. Above, an elaborate crystal chandelier provided candle light. There were two fireplaces in the room and tall windows lining the walls. Displayed in the room were a British drum, swords, and flag captured in 1775 by Continental Army soldiers under the command of Ethan Allan at the battle of Fort Ticonderoga.

The detail of the description gives it a sense of accuracy that helps transport the reader to the physical location, the very room in which the Declaration was made. For many readers it must have an air of familiarity about it since Marcovitz is essentially describing the image millions have seen in the Capitol, the image with which I began. A painting which itself is clothed in the rhetoric of authenticity and historical exactitude: Trumbull, as the evidence of his correspondence and sketches demonstrates, went to extreme pains to produce a documentary image. He travelled across the states tracking down those people who had been present on 4 July 1776 in that room in Philadelphia in order accurately to portray their faces in his painting. Of course, his subjects had advanced in years by the time Trumbull came with pencil, pen or brush in hand – he did not begin his studies for the painting in Paris until 1785 and it was not completed until 1818. No wonder so many of them look so august. Similarly the room he positioned them in, with its drum, swords, flags and doorways, is presented to us as an accurate depiction of the Assembly Room in the State House. But when he began his initial sketches of the composition for the painting in the company of Thomas Jefferson – in fact it was Jefferson who had suggested the subject for the painting – he had never visited Philadelphia. He was, therefore, completely reliant upon the sketch of the room that Jefferson made for him, and as we now know Jefferson had misremembered many of the details, including the positions of the doorways and the adornments to the walls. Trumbull, in a later version of the same painting, took great care to correct these errors.

Leaving aside the accuracy of the depiction of the room, Marcovitz's narrative then moves into what transpired that day:

> At the front of the room stood the president's *dais* – a raised table and chair usually occupied by the speaker of the Pennsylvania Assembly. On July 4, 1776, delegate John Hancock of Massachusetts sat at that table, having been named president of the Congress by the other delegates.

Hancock dropped the gavel to open the debate. One by one, delegates from the 13 colonies took turns making their arguments on independence.

Then, following a preamble about the discussions held on the days leading up to the Fourth, he states that 'the declaration was read'. Finally, after further discussion and changes to the document that Jefferson and his committee had submitted, 'a roll call vote was taken' in which 'all delegates but those representing New York cast their ballots for independence'. Then, Marcovitz states, came the moment which for a complex set of reasons discussed in the chapters following essentially marks the beginning of the nation: the document was signed. 'At first' he writes, 'the declaration received just two signatures – those of Hancock, the president of the Congress, and Charles Thomson, the secretary.' Later – how much later he does not say – ' the signatures of the other delegates were added'.

This can be said to be the kernel of the story of the Fourth of July. Although some people today, be they Americans or citizens of other countries, might struggle to capture much of its detail – indeed they may even have forgotten why celebrations take place that day – very few would contest the basic fact that the Declaration of Independence was made on 4 July 1776. There are countless representations of this fact and the painting with which I began provides evidence of a kind for it. Yet if we view events with a little more historical information at our disposal and with a cool, keen eye we can begin to see some of the multiple threads woven throughout the story this book tells which might cast doubt on what is commonly perceived.

Is Trumbull's image really presenting a moment to us and,

if so, can we be certain which moment it might be? It may be the case, for example, that the artist did not have in mind the depiction of a single moment at all; he might have set out to conflate a number of significant moments as he struggled to produce an iconic image to fit the brief Congress had given him. But let us leave this possibility aside in order to see how Trumbull's painting might be read as recording either of two quite different acts which are part of the history of the document we know as the Declaration of Independence. On the one hand it might be depicting the first time that Jefferson and his four accomplices presented to Congress the draft they had prepared of that document. This took place on 28 June. Since the five-man team that was the drafting committee occupies the centre of the image it might be understood in this way. But in the subsequent history of the Declaration no one has ever made a strong case for the significance of 28 June, so it would seem improbable that Trumbull intended to depict *that* moment.

It is much more likely that the artist, in discussion with Jefferson in Paris in 1785, began to formulate how he might depict the moment which, even by then, had come to be seen as a defining moment in the history of American independence, the moment at which the Declaration *was signed*. And this, as everyone knows, took place on 4 July. This would seem to be a more plausible account of what we see. It explains why Jefferson is depicted gesturing with his left hand, pointing to the place at the bottom of the document where the man seated on the other side of the table, John Hancock, was supposed to sign his name.

In the document we now know as The Declaration of Independence (illustration 2), Hancock left his signature to history and in the process bequeathed a figure of speech

2. *The first signature on the document we know as the Declaration of Independence was that of the chairman of the Second Continental Congress, John Hancock. Much has been made of the fact that it is larger than all the others.*

used to refer to the mark we call a signature: a 'Hancock'. But if Trumbull's painting depicts what happened on 4 July, Jefferson cannot be holding the document since that was made only later under instruction from Congress in a resolution of 19 July 1776. Furthermore, there is no record of the signatories to that sheet of parchment ever coming together as a body in the room depicted by Trumbull for the express purpose of signing the document now preserved in the State Archives in Washington, DC. Nevertheless, millions of viewers of the painting believe they have seen, frozen in time, the moment at which the declaration was made, and what is understood by 'making' the declaration is, naturally and effortlessly, assumed to be the same thing as signing the document. Much of this book is about how that came to be.

If many of the faces around the outer edges of the room are only now familiar to historians and *amateurs* of the revolutionary period, the group in the centre of the painting depicts at least three men who have subsequently become heroic actors in the story of the formation of the republic.

Known to us as Founding Fathers, they were instrumental in the birth of modern America. At the left of the group is John Adams, the second president of the United States and one of the most important figures in the colonial struggle for independence. He was forty-one in 1776 and had by that time made his reputation in Massachusetts as a lawyer and a man of considerable learning. He did not mince his words and argued his case with passion and energy. Within his own lifetime he was dubbed the 'Atlas of American Independence'.

At the far right is Benjamin Franklin, perhaps the most variously talented and gifted of all those who played a role in the founding of the nation. He was the oldest signatory of the Declaration, well into his seventieth year in July 1776. Printer, member of the Assembly in Pennsylvania, scientist and diplomat, Franklin's humour and intelligence were indelibly scored across the political debates which eventually brought independence to the colonies.

And heading the group, standing in closest proximity to the table and holding the document he was to come to think of as his own property, is Thomas Jefferson. This book, and the story of the founding of America that it tells, would be completely different, almost impossible to tell, without him.

1

THE FOURTH OF JULY 1776:

THE EVENT AND THE MYTH

PHILADELPHIA, 4 JULY 1776

It wasn't, in the overall scheme of things, such a big deal. The weather all summer had been sticky but rarely swelteringly hot. Conditions had been a little different inside the chamber of the State House in which the Second Continental Congress held its meetings since sessions were held with windows closed and doors locked to prevent anyone overhearing the deliberations. On the morning of the 4th, at 6.00 a.m., Thomas Jefferson recorded that the temperature was 68 degrees Fahrenheit. There was a modest south-easterly breeze and it looked as if it would be another humid day, although the future third president noted in his diary that he distrusted his thermometer and needed to buy a new one.

About fifty delegates to the Congress were in Philadelphia that day – the exact number is not known – those from Pennsylvania, not surprisingly, outnumbering the representatives from the other twelve colonies. Some of the most important spokesmen for independence, such as Richard Henry Lee and George Wythe, had left the city nearly a month earlier on 13 June. The previous day, on the 12th, Congress had appointed yet another committee – this one to draft proposals for a putative confederal structure for the thirteen colonies.

Independence was in the air, though no one at that moment could have predicted precisely when the majority of delegates from each colony would finally sign up for separation. Some of them, such as John Adams, had been gasping for the ratification of what they believed to be inevitable for months. Others were only slowly coming round to accepting the final and decisive step into a new era. And then there were those delegates whose personal or professional lives were in the immediate term taking their full attention: Oliver Wolcott from Connecticut, for example, had left Philadelphia on account of illness. Some, like Lewis Morris, the tall, handsome Yale-educated aristocrat from New York, had to deal with local crises back in their home towns or colonies – Morris had been called away to take command of a local militia. There was, then, no sense that 4 July would become, in the words of John Adams, the 'epochal' moment. Those who remained in Philadelphia rose early since the meeting was scheduled to begin at 9.00 a.m. and the agenda was lengthy. No one doubted that these were dangerous times.

Uppermost in everyone's mind was the intelligence that had arrived five days earlier: around a hundred and fifty of His Majesty's ships had been sighted off Sandy Hook, New Jersey. For some time now, it had been clear to the Committee of Safety that the strength of individual militias in each colony would not be sufficient to repel the forces of the British. They had, therefore, recommended to Congress that a 'flying camp' be formed. This was to comprise the various town militias from a number of colonies which could move swiftly to wherever a military crisis seemed imminent.

It was fortunate that Congress had adopted this recommendation without too much debate since the current situation was becoming critical. For – on the morning of 3 July – news was abroad that the fleet had landed on Staten Island. Most of the delegates reasoned that an immediate attempt on New York was likely to be deemed too hazardous by His Majesty's forces and, this being so, the most proximate colonies of Pennsylvania and New Jersey would become prime targets. As day broke on the 4th the four men who served on the Committee of Safety – Benjamin Franklin, Robert Livingston, Francis Hopkinson and John Dickinson – knew they would have to assess the risk of imminent hostilities within the colony and recommend a course of action to their colleagues. And each delegate knew that the committee's proposals would undoubtedly be the main business of the day.

And so it proved to be. The four men met with great urgency. One of their number, Livingston, was instructed to draft a letter to the Lancaster Associators setting out the plan to form a flying camp. A second committee, the Committee of Inspection chaired by Thomas McKean, a young lawyer from Delaware, also met that day and conferred with the field officers who were in Philadelphia. During the afternoon of 4 July Congress ratified the letters that each of these committees proposed and instructed that they be printed as a single document and dispatched by rider to Lancaster. This was the only official written communication issued by Congress that day. It begins:

Gentlemen,
The congress this morning directed us to confer with the Committees of Safety and Inspection, and the Field

Officers now in town, about the proper mode of collecting the militia of this province, in order to form a flying camp, to cover Pennsylvania and New-Jersey, from the Attacks of the Enemy, who have landed on Staten-Island, and will probably direct their March this Way, if they should imagine the Attempt on New-York too hazardous.

It is true that some business from two days earlier needed to be dealt with. At the conclusion of the discussion of the draft declaration which had begun on 1 July it had become clear that unanimity was now in sight and the resolution beginning 'these colonies are, and of right ought to be, free and independent States ...' was likely to be passed. But by the end of the long second day, Tuesday 2 July, it was still unclear as to how this intention to signal the colonists' separation from the mother country ought to be broadcast and acted upon. This was to take up the first hour or so of business on the 4th. By 11.00 a.m., the entire thing was done and dusted. A local printer by the name of John Dunlap was to be instructed to print up the text they had approved two days earlier and instructions for its public dissemination were to be sent to the various colonies and to the army that was under the direction of George Washington. Then discussion of a further fourteen items of business commenced. The noble and revered passage which begins 'When in the course of human events ...' was not proclaimed from the steps of the State House. No bells rang. No fireworks were sent into the blue sky. It was another Thursday in the long march towards independence. That was it.

It must be said that throughout the summer the idea of

revolution had been gently simmering away. The delegates collected together in Philadelphia had been pushing around the arguments for and against 'independency' for months. Some, like John Dickinson, a brilliant lawyer from Pennsylvania, were yet to be convinced that complete separation at this moment was timely, and these men, though certainly not loyalists, kept open the possibility of voting against independence right up to the last. But by the turn of June into July there were too many now minded to embark upon the adventure of what would come to be seen as the first truly modern republic. And although no one was in any doubt about the danger of separation, or in any doubt about the illegality of it according to the laws in place in each of the colonies, most were also now firmly committed to the revolution in government that the firebrands had been promoting since the Stamp Act eleven years earlier. Trepidation and excitement in equal measure were certainly in the air in Philadelphia that summer in 1776, so when it was finally done, when all the colonies excepting New York, which had abstained in the crucial vote on 2 July, voted for independence there was some cause for celebration. At least to those who were now sold on the idea of creating a new nation. But of course throughout the colonies, for reasons of vested interest, sentimental attachment to the mother country, dyed-in-the-wool loyalty to authority and tradition or just plain fear of the consequences of embarking upon what could still be regarded as a treasonable act, many remained opposed to the hotheads in Philadelphia. Above all else we must remember that in 1776, on 4 July, the outcome of the declaration seeking to announce the intention to 'dissolve the political bands' which had, heretofore, connected one people with another was unknown.

For those like John Adams, who had been advocating separation for so long and whose views were a matter of public record, the vote on 2 July was the culmination of years of persuasion and debate. Even those delegates like John Witherspoon, the president of the College of New Jersey at Princeton, who came late to the political struggle were now fully convinced that it was time to seize the day. Witherspoon, who was said to be one of the very few men of his era whose influence or force of presence rivalled that of Washington himself, had risen to his feet on 2 July to support the move for independence by claiming that the country was 'not only ripe for the measure but in danger of rotting for the want of it'. So yes, there was reason for celebration when the die was finally cast *on 2 July*.

But even then, on that rather hotter Tuesday when the Congress had once more rehearsed the arguments, now all too familiar to everyone, the decision felt anticlimactic. At least it did to John Adams, who wrote to his wife the next day: 'Had a Declaration of Independency been made seven Months ago, it would have been attended with many great and glorious effects … We might before this Hour, have formed Alliances with foreign States.' For Adams the cost of delaying the decision had been significant. It had, for example, resulted in the loss of Canada for the Union. Notwithstanding these differences of opinion he nevertheless rather grudgingly granted that the slow process had also had its advantages: 'time has been given for the whole People' he wrote in the same letter, 'maturely to consider the great Question of Independence and to ripen their Judgments, dissipate their Fears and allure their Hopes, by discussing it, in Assemblies, Conventions, Committees of Safety and Inspection, in Town and County Meetings, as well as in private Conversations, so that the whole People in every Colony of the 13, have now adopted it, as their own Act.'

As far as Adams was concerned the progress leading towards independence had not been particularly smooth. There had been moments when the general drift in the direction of independence got stuck, and then others when it looked more likely. But although he had lived the political process which resulted in an act that was to be decisive, he would have been hard pressed to say when, exactly, that process had come to its resolution: On 1 July, when the debate at last came formally to the Congress? Or the following day at the conclusion of that debate? Adams had not doubted the outcome for weeks. As far as he was concerned the only remaining impediment was the slow progress towards unanimity of all thirteen colonies.

But history, in the sense of *what happened*, always comes to us in the form of punctual moments – *this* happened on *that* day at *that* hour in *this* place, and so on. When we attempt to reconstruct the sequence and consequence of past events it is inevitable that history seems to be full of such decisive moments. But there are many kinds of 'event' in history. Those of a cataclysmic kind, such as an earthquake or the beheading of a monarch, can be precisely dated, even timed. One might say that their temporality is that of the instrument we use for registering the spinning of the earth on its axis: the clock. But most of those things we like to think of as 'historical events' are not like this, and as we know from our own lived experience these kinds of events have a different kind of temporality. When we look at them closely we see that they have no singular moment of 'happening'. In the sense that 4 July 1776 was an 'event', that something happened that day which by long tradition is celebrated each year, it can be said *never to have never happened*. It is a peculiar, though not unique, kind of historical event and this book tells its story.

While it is certainly true that something connected to the Declaration of Independence *did* happen on 4 July 1776 in Philadelphia, it is also true that from that day to this the celebration that is entered into on the Fourth is not of *that*. For what happened that day in Congress was the agreement to print and publish the Declaration whose form of words had first been presented two days earlier. But, as we shall see below, even if a case can be made for assigning the 'punctuality' of the event to 2 July, there are problems here too. In fact, once we begin to trace carefully the origin of any political act, the idea that there might be a *moment* at which such acts come into being begins to feel like sand in the outstretched palm of the hand. *This* decision may have been taken at *that* time – even precisely date- and time-stamped – but then that decision is revealed as being built upon or implied by an earlier one, and so on.

Of course, it might be said in riposte to this kind of thinking that we are merely splitting hairs, or standing too much on an obstructive principle of accuracy. So what if the Declaration was actually made two days earlier? Surely the point of the celebrations on the 4th is to mark the moment at which a new nation came into being. Or to honour and reaffirm the principles upon which that new nation was founded. And this is undoubtedly so. But there is also a more interesting story to be told. For what the history of the tradition of the Fourth allows us to see is the past and present significance of the celebratory act. Furthermore, it brings into sharp focus the fact that honouring the Fourth *does* something; it is not, in itself, an inert political act. Thus, as will become evident, although the moment of the Declaration was to those who lived through the time of its enunciation a matter of no real importance, the fact that subsequently it became possible to claim that it was a *punctual moment*, and moreover that its significance substantially lies in that *punctuality*, has become one of the most important features of its continuing political resonance. The claim, indeed the belief, that the Declaration happened at a stroke, as it were, when the words of the document were first enunciated provides the scaffolding for a new kind of political agency. A republic whose legitimating institution is the collective speaking as one: we the people.

John Adams, as we have seen, thought that the final debates were nothing more than pro forma. Writing to Samuel Chase on 1 July he reported that the first day of the momentous discussion was 'an idle mispence of time, for nothing was said but what had been repeated and hackneyed in that room before, a hundred times, for six months past'. But even he fell into the rhetoric of the *punctual*, recognising that even if the movement towards separation from Britain and the consequent foundation of a new political entity was now inevitable, this first step into an uncertain future nevertheless needed its moment of ratification. So, on the same day that he wrote to his wife in terms effectively saying 'no big deal – we should have done it months ago', he also says:

Yesterday the greatest Question was decided, which was ever debated in America, and a greater perhaps, never was or will be decided among Men. A Resolution was passed without one dissenting Colony, 'that these united Colonies, are, and of right ought to be free and independ-

ent States, and as such, they have, and of Right ought
to have full Power to make War, conclude Peace, establish Commerce, and to do all the other Acts and Things,
which other States may rightfully do'.

And then in a second letter the same day, obviously
having had some time to mull things over, air his sense of
frustration, commiserate perhaps with some of his colleagues
from Massachusetts over the length of time it had taken, he
eventually finds a residue of energy and excitement. 'But the
Day is past', he reflects on the struggle to achieve unanimity, 'the Second Day of July 1776, will be the most memorable Epocha, in the History of America'. Then, warming to
his theme: 'I am apt to believe that it will be celebrated, by
succeeding Generations, as the great anniversary Festival. It
ought to be solemnized with Pomp and Parade, with Shews,
Games, Sports, Guns, Bells, Bonfires and Illuminations from
one End of this Continent to the other from this Time forward
forever more.' Well, he may have got the day wrong, but he
was pretty firmly on the button with everything else. Just
how prescient will become clear as we follow the invention
and adoption of the various rituals comprising the tradition
of celebration that is the Fourth.

But if Adams thought that 2 July marked the *moment* at
which the course of human history changed, others who had
also lived through the weeks, months and years of political debate felt the pressure of different moments along the
way. Congress had met on 28 June to read the draft of the
Declaration that had been prepared by Thomas Jefferson, and
the consideration of the text that day can, to some extent, be
said to mark the moment when separation from the mother
country moved from the hypothetical to the realizable. We

do not know what was said once Congress formed itself as the 'Committee of the Whole' since no minutes of these meetings were taken. But we do know that the draft prepared by Jefferson was altered and that on 28 June Congress decided to postpone its ratification of the document for another three days. So expectations were already building about the potential significance for the *first* of July, the day when the matter, it was thought, would be resolved. John Penn, one of the many delegates who practised law when in his home colony, in his case North Carolina, wrote from Philadelphia on 28 June:

> The first day of July will be an era of great importance as that is the day for debating the great and important question of Independance and from what I have seen there is no doubt but a total separation between Britain and her Colonies, that were, will take place as all the Provinces but Maryland are for it, and the Inhabitants there are coming over fast. I fear most people are too sanguine relative to commerce, however it is a measure our enemies have forced upon us. I don't doubt but we shall have spirit enough to act like men, indeed it could no longer be delayed.

As things turned out it took another day to get to the actual resolution, but many of those present recognised that by the end of Monday 1 July it was a fait accompli. This was certainly the view of the man who is said to have cast the first vote for independence, Josiah Bartlett, a physician from New Hampshire. He had written from Philadelphia to John Langdon on 1 July: 'The affair of Independency has been this day determined in a Committee of the Whole; by next Post I expect you will receive a formal declaration with the reasons …' So a case could be mounted for proposing 1 July as the significant punctual moment, especially given the fact that notwithstanding the secrecy which surrounded the deliberations of the Committee of the whole – or at least its desire to prevent anything incriminating getting into the record – it would appear that the entire city was aware of what was happening. As the 32-year-old Elbridge Gerry, one of the Massachusetts delegation, wrote to James Warren on 2 July: 'I have only time to inform you that yesterday was agitated in Congress the great question of Independency'. But this, he makes clear, was hardly a secret: 'as the facts are well known at the Coffee-House of the city as in Congress, I may go on to inform you that, in a Committee of the whole House, it was carried by nine Colonies'. Surely it is reasonable to assume that if the talk of the coffee houses had been this explicit it would have been likely for such intelligence to spread far and wide, its progress determined merely by the speed at which a horse and rider might travel between towns across the colonies.

If a case for the decisive moment can be made for the Monday or Tuesday of the first week in July it begins to erode the sense one might hold on to that a political act of this kind has a *precise origin*. Just as the debate that took place on 1 July – not conclusive in a technical sense, but nevertheless definitive in outline and consequence – had been proleptically signalled at the meeting on 28 June, so that meeting had been foreseen by the earlier resolution made on 10 June which states 'that the consideration of the first resolution [regarding separation] be postponed to this day, three weeks [i.e. 1 July] …' Although at this time a number of colonies had yet fully to instruct their delegates to vote in favour of the resolution, it is clear from the journal of the Congress that the drift was towards a declaration of independence, since on that day, 10 June, it is recorded that Congress also agreed that 'a committee be appointed to prepare a declaration to the effect of the said first resolution, which is in these words: "That these United Colonies are, and of right ought to be, free and independent states ..."'. And the next day it is recorded that Congress duly appointed a five-man committee with instructions to draft a document expressing the colonists' desire to separate from the mother country. It could be argued that *in setting up such a committee to draft the document* the move towards independence had in effect been decided.

But, again, the appointment on 11 June of Jefferson, Adams, Franklin, Sherman and Livingston to a drafting committee with instructions to draw up the document that was to become the first text of the new nation was itself the outcome of a discussion held three days earlier, on 7 June. It is, in fact, on this day that for the first time independence can be said to have been within the reach of the colonists as an achievable political act. Since we do not know what was said on the day Richard Henry Lee got to his feet and proposed, under instruction from the Virginia convention, 'that these United Colonies, are, and of right ought to be, free and independent states: that they are absolved from all allegiance to the British Crown; and that all political connection between them and the state of Great Britain is, and ought to be, totally dissolved' – words that were inserted by Congress into Jefferson's final paragraph of the document that is now revered as his – we can nevertheless surmise that, since further discussion of his proposal was postponed so that delegates could return to their colonies in order to ascertain the measure of support for such a bold step, it must have been the case that a significant number of delegates present on 7 June *were* minded to vote for independence. It could be said, then, that the *decisive* moment was on 7 June.

The first time the text of the Declaration was, in a simple sense, 'declared' in public occurred on 8 July when a member of the Committee of Safety – probably John Nixon – stood in the State House yard and read the document aloud to a large crowd of people. According to John Adams cheers rose up, the battalions paraded on the common and fired into the air. He claimed that 'the bells rang all day and almost all night'. And so the tradition of celebration that was to become The Fourth of July began, on 8 July.

THE FOURTH OF JULY 1776

History tells a different story. At least the history which has become woven into the fabric of the nation's founding promotes a rather more climactic version of what happened that day. Although the account of events that follows is certainly inaccurate as far as we are able to reconstruct them, it is also, simultaneously, an accurate rendition of the myth that, through repeated telling over the stretch of time between then and now, millions of Americans have learnt as the truth. It is a story that helps one come to an understanding of an extremely complex political and conceptual event: the birth of a nation. Even if, as shall become clear, the notion that nations have singular moments of birth is recognised as suspect it nevertheless remains the case that without the transforming aid of narrative, history in the sense of what happened remains inert, beyond or beside the reach of understanding.

In point of fact, to this day most Americans believe that the celebrations on the Fourth do not commemorate the moment when the Declaration was made, howsoever that might be understood, but the act of *signing* the document itself. That this is so tells us something about the power of the signature and its assumed guarantee of veracity. It is not enough, in a curious way, that the words of the Declaration might have been spoken at a particular moment – in the State House, outside in the yard, from the steps of meeting halls all over the colonies. For what seals the authenticity of the origin, what allows it to be elevated to the status of *the* moment of origin, is the fact of the signature. And, given that this was a collective act – Congress issued the document we know as the Declaration of Independence – it requires more than one signature. At least its declaratory power would be diminished were it to have been signed by only one person, say John Hancock, the president of the Second Continental Congress, even if he was the delegated representative of that body. Consequently, as we know, 4 July was the day on which fifty-five members of the Congress that was to secure the fate of the colonies *signed* the declaration (a fifty-sixth, John Dickinson, having declined to add his signature).

It is true to say that the record of the Congress is itself contradictory on this point, but for reasons that will be explained below it is relatively easy to reconcile the discrepancies. In any case it is very unlikely that the various versions of these early congressional meetings, with minutes and resolutions taken in something approaching Masonic code, kick-started the story that has been learnt by millions. It is almost certain that the source of the claim that the Declaration was signed on 4 July is to be found in the writings of Jefferson, who stated in a letter written to S. A. Wells on 12 May 1819 that he had kept notes throughout the meetings in Philadelphia during the summer of '76. These were subsequently written up in his own Journals at a distance of time that is unknown. Jefferson's notes, as preserved, are in fact pretty sketchy but it is the following entry that gave birth to the story countless generations of Americans have passed down as lore. Jefferson states: 'The debates having taken up the greater parts of the 2d, 3d and 4th days of July, were, in the evening of the last, closed;' and he continues 'the declaration was reported by the commee [sic], agreed to by the house; and signed by every member except mr. Dickinson.'

Jefferson was writing to Wells seven years before he died, and at that time, late in life with his posthumous reputation much in mind, he was vigorously constructing a platform to support the edifice that was to become his legacy and memorial: Thomas Jefferson, author of the Declaration of Independence. He was also remembering events that happened forty-three years earlier. There is a great deal of evidence, albeit some of it circumstantial, pointing to the conclusion that on 4 July, 1776 no signatures were appended to any document. But even if they were it is most likely that only two, those of the president and secretary of the Congress, were appended below the text following the standard format for all the documents that were issued by Congress at the time. As we have already seen, the discussion on the 4th resulted in an instruction given to John Dunlap to print the words that were now agreed, but it has never been claimed that this material document (such as it may have been) or any of its copies is *the* Declaration. That honour belongs to a subsequent artefact, the piece of parchment on which the words were inscribed as per the resolution Congress made on 19 July. And we know for certain that *this document* was subsequently signed since it survives to the present day and may be inspected in the National Archives. But even this may not be the original or first signed document. The *Journals of Congress* refer to a 'comparison' of the parchment copy, but to what is not recorded.

On 6 August 1822, Jefferson, having just received a copy of the printed *Journals of Congress* (they had remained confidential until that year), added a marginal comment to his copy of a letter he had sent to S. A. Wells three years before. Jefferson, as is well known, was fastidious in his correspondence, having invented a copying machine which allowed him to keep multiple copies of letters he penned, and kept not only the replies to his letters but also copies of his own. In this addendum to the original letter sent to Wells on 12 May 1819, prompted by what he had just read in the record of Congress's meetings, Jefferson claimed that the 'comparison' mentioned in the *Journals* was between the parchment and a paper version of the same document. Furthermore, there is an implication that both included the signatures of the delegates. Unfortunately there is no corroborating evidence for what Jefferson referred to as the 'original signed on paper' anywhere in the substantial archive of letters, papers, minutes, or journals of any of the key players of 4 July 1776.

And in point of fact, already by the turn of the century as the story of the nation was being refined and remade, the veracity of the account in the printed *Journals of Congress* of what happened on 4 July in the State House in Philadelphia had been questioned. One of the delegates to the Congress, Thomas McKean from Delaware, was first to raise the alarm in a letter to Alexander James Dallas of 26 September 1796. In the course of this correspondence he questions whether the public record does, in fact, get the matter right. He wrote:

'By the printed publications referred to it would appear as if the fifty-five Gentlemen, whose names are there printed and none other, were on that day personally present in Congress and assenting the declaration: Whereas the truth is otherwise.' It has been suggested that the origin of this inaccuracy lays in the misreading of both the printed *Journals* and Jefferson's own notes, taken during the meeting and subsequently written up. But a careful reading of the printed Congress *Journals* indicates that a blank space was left at the time of writing up the meeting of 4 July so that at a later date the full text of the Declaration, with signatures, could be inserted. When it came to printing up the *Journals* the document, which by then had been in the public domain for over forty years – the vellum with its impressive looking legal handwriting – provided the text complete with signatures. And we know that the vellum document was made following the resolution passed on 19 July 1776 by the Second Continental Congress which indicates that it was to be signed by all the delegates. If, as Jefferson claimed, a different paper version was also signed the *Journals* are silent on the matter.

As for the misreading of Jefferson's note it has been claimed that Jefferson did not mean to imply that the document was signed *at the conclusion* of the debate, on the evening of 4 July. Rather, so it is said, his last clause indicating that it was signed 'by every member except mr. Dickinson' gives no indication as to *when* those signatures were appended. Whatever we make of these corrections and counter-claims it remains the case that the common understanding of the events of 4 July has it that the document was signed by the fifty-five assenting delegates that day. This we know to be false. As Thomas McKean's letter continues: 'The following Gentlemen were not Members of Congress on the 4th day

of July, 1776, namely, Mathew Thornton, Benjamin Rush,
George Clymer, James Smith, George Taylor and George
Ross: the last five named were not chosen Delegates until
the 20th day of the Month, the first not until the 12th day of
September following, nor did he take his seat in Congress
until the 4th of November, which was four Months after.'

These are correct statements. Although each of the five
Pennsylvania delegates voted into Congress on 20 July were
proud to sign the document after they took their seats, the
record indicates that they were not present for the debate
which concluded with the order to print the document we
know as The Declaration of Independence. And, to make
matters worse, at least for Thomas McKean, the relevant
volume of the printed *Journals of Congress* was also inaccurate in its omissions. As McKean writes:

> Modesty should not rob any man of his just honour,
> when by that honour his modesty cannot be offended.
> My name is not in the printed Journals of Congress as
> party to the declaration of Independence, and this, like
> an error in the first concoction, has vitiated most of the
> subsequent publications; and yet the fact is, that I was
> then a member of Congress for the State of Delaware,
> was personally present in Congress and voted in favour
> of independence on the 4th day of July 1776, and signed
> the declaration after it had been engrossed on parchment,
> where my name in my own hand writing still appears.

Of course McKean's correction, made as it was at the end
of the eighteenth century, could easily have fallen into the
inner recesses of the archive where it might have languished
forever more. But in 1922 Carl Becker published a book that

was to become a standard source for the history of the era – *The Declaration of Independence: A Study in the History of Political Ideas* – in which he pointed out in very direct language that 'Contrary to a tradition early established and long held, the Declaration was not signed by the members of Congress on July 4th'. Becker was himself drawing on the work of John Hazelton, published as *The Declaration of Independence: its History* in 1906; it is a curious fact, however, that from 1922 until 1978, when Garry Wills published *Inventing America: Jefferson's Declaration of Independence*, scholarship by and large turned a blind eye to the intricate history of the nation's founding document. And even though one would have imagined that the story about the events of 4 July 1776 would by now have come closer to the facts exhibited in this scholarship it nevertheless remains the case that Jefferson's version of events – or at least one interpretation of his version – holds sway.

If one consults what might be regarded as the official site of the nation, the White House website, the current Bush administration makes no mention of the signing, preferring to make a different claim about the significance of the day. It reads: 'On 4th July, 1776, we claimed our independence from Britain and Democracy was born.' There are other stories in this brief sketch of what happened in 1776 with piles just as deeply driven into the sea bed of the nation's founding ideology: the notion of right compacted within the formulation 'we claimed ...' for example, or that Democracy was born on July 4th, 1776. But it is out of step with the 130 million websites which contain 'July 4th' on their pages, many of them devoted to telling the story of the nation's founding. One, entitled 'Happy Birthday America' states:

Welcome to Independence Day on the Net.

Independence day celebrates the birthday of the United States of America. Founded July 4th 1776, with the signing of the Declaration of Independence America is celebrating its 230th birthday this year (2006).

So why does this myth of the Fourth continue to have currency? Why, even in the face of good clear evidence to the contrary, does it seem attractive to believe that on 4 July 1776 America was born? Of course, nations do not have singular moments of origin any more than any other complex political events do. The answer to that question can be understood only in the context of the historical tradition of celebration that makes the Fourth of July a present and continuing act with political significance. An act with deep and continuing connections to the project that is America. Even if the selection of the day itself, the 4th, cannot sustain the weight that has subsequently been placed upon it one should nevertheless hold on to the fact that *something* took place on that day which now symbolically stands for a *punctual moment* that never was. Furthermore, it is salutary to remember that the aspirations given voice in the act of declaring independence, whenever that transpired, are not only noble but have yet to be fully achieved. And this – America's destiny – announced by those who count themselves among the number making a declaration of intent, to hold certain truths self-evident, is worth celebrating.

DECLARATIONS OF INDEPENDENCE

Sometime in June 1775 Captain James Jack set out from Charlotte, North Carolina, for Philadelphia. He was riding 'express', as quickly as he could, since he had been instructed to carry news of the Declaration of Independence made by the citizens of Mecklenburg County on 20 May to the Second Continental Congress that was then meeting in Philadelphia. The town he had left could not, in today's terms, be called substantial. Fewer than a hundred people lived within the town limits. Only one of the houses was painted and almost all of the others were little more than log cabins. The courthouse, which stood on pillars twelve feet above the marketplace, was also of log construction, and it had a porch at the front entrance which was approached up a flight of steps.

There were some rudimentary amenities around the central square. Nicholson's was a tavern, as was Pat Jack's. There was a general store and a jail but not much else. Charlotte was, however, the centre for the community in the county of Mecklenburg which was home to seven Presbyterian congregations scattered around the outlying country. Their names evoke the local scenery: Sugaw Creek, Poplar Tent, Rocky River, Steele Creek. In all around 7,000 people inhabited the county and the homes of many were to be found on small plantations. The roads were narrow and most of the countryside remained uncultivated with thick woods dominating the landscape.

By far the greater number of the local families had their origins in Northern Ireland, from where the Ulster–Scottish Presbyterian community had begun emigrating to the colonies around 1684. They were proud of their heritage and reluctant to bow to the dictates arriving at regular intervals from London. One recent aggravation had been caused by the Vestry and Marriage Acts passed in 1769. This had imposed fines of five pounds on Presbyterian ministers if they chose to conduct marriage ceremonies. By the time of the Mecklenburg convention in 1775 most of the town elders – almost exclusively ministers in the Scottish church – were implacably set against the governor, William Tyron, and his political masters back in England.

On the day set aside for the meeting – 19 May – an express rider arrived in Charlotte bringing news of the engagements between British forces and the colonists at Lexington and Concord that had occurred a month earlier. The meeting was scheduled for the evening, and had been called by Colonel Thomas Polk, the founder of Charlotte. Twenty-six men convened, two delegates from every militia company in the county supplemented by a few other dignitaries. It was chaired by Abraham Alexander, and John McKnitt Alexander, a 42-year-old planter and surveyor, acted as clerk. They met through the night, finally coming to a resolution at 2.00 a.m. on Saturday 20 May. Later that day, at noon, the town's founder stood on the courthouse steps and read aloud the resolutions they had made. He began: 'That whosoever directly or indirectly abetted or in any way, form or manner countenanced the unchartered & dangerous invasion of our rights as claimed by G. Britain is an enemy to this County – to America & to the inherent & inalienable rights of man.' These words were undoubtedly prompted by the extreme indignation the citizens of Mecklenburg felt for their fellow colonists in Massachusetts who had, just one month before, suffered an invasion from His Majesty's troops. And having been prompted to their declaration of solidarity they began to warm to the theme of independence. The second resolve began: 'We the Citizens of Mecklenburg County do hereby dissolve the political bands which have connected us to the Mother Country ...' and then, in the third resolution, the principle upon which the colonies were to stake their future was declared:

> That we do hereby declare ourselves a free and independent people; are, and of right ought to be, a sovereign and self-governing Association, under the control of no power other than that of our God and the general government of the Congress; to the maintenance of which independence, we solemnly pledge to each other our mutual co-operation, our lives, our fortunes, and our most sacred honor.

Among those who had been charged with the responsibility of drafting the document was William Kennon, a lawyer from the town of Salisbury, forty miles to the north. Kennon had been born in Virginia, where he also received his legal training, before moving to Rowan County. And it was Kennon who greeted Captain Jack when he arrived in Salisbury sometime in early June on his way to deliver the news of Mecklenburg's declaration of independence to the Second Continental Congress. After a brief delay Jack continued his express ride northwards, arriving in Philadelphia sometime before 23 June when Washington left the city to take command of the army, then outside Boston. And at some point in the days immediately preceding the 23rd Jack delivered his document to at least two of the three North Carolina delegates, Richard Caswell, Joseph Hewes and William Hooper, who had been in Philadelphia all summer.

For forty-five years this obscure event in colonial American history lay buried in the memories of its protagonists. The course of history had not seen fit to include the story of how the citizens of Mecklenburg County had pre-empted the declaration announced on 4 July 1776 by over a year. But then, on 5 June 1819, the *Essex Register*, a local Massachusetts paper, reprinted an account of the Mecklenburg resolves which had appeared two months earlier in the 30 April edition of the *Raleigh Register and North Carolina Gazette*. The ageing John Adams read his copy of the *Essex Register* with amazement and wrote promptly to his old rival Thomas Jefferson with whom, in later life, he had become reconciled: 'How is it possible that this paper should have been concealed from me to this day? he asked, continuing, 'Had it been communicated to me in the time of it, I know, if you do not know, that it would have been printed in every Whig News-paper upon this Continent.' Adams then has some fun by suggesting that if such a declaration had been known about at the time he would have capitalised on the fact: 'You know if I had possessed it, I would have made the Hall of Congress Echo and re-echo, with it fifteen Months before your Declaration of Independence.'

In reply Jefferson was adamant that the Mecklenburg story was just that, a story put about by proud North Carolinians: '... what has attracted my peculiar notice is the paper from Mecklenburg County of N. Carolina, published in the Essex Register ... you seem to think it genuine. I believe it spurious.' By the second decade of the nineteenth century the revolutionary war was far enough in the past, and the sense of future security sufficient for various rivalries to emerge in relation to the respective roles individual colonies had played in the founding of the nation. And few were as proud of their history of resistance and independence as North Carolina. Jefferson, the proud Virginian, had his own loyalties. He may have felt the way he did about North Carolina on account of his opinion of the three delegates from the colony at the Second Continental Congress, none of whom played a significant role in the proceedings of that body. But within the local context of the colony and subsequent state there were many heroes who had stood firm for the rights of the colonists. And their number included both Thomas Polk and John McKnitt Alexander.

It may have been the case that Adams also remained sceptical about the Mecklenburg initiative, for he too had a reputation and a proud colonial affiliation to protect. He did, after all, give Jefferson an escape route by suggesting that such intelligence could never have been concealed from the two most prominent members of the drafting committee for Congress's own declaration. But, even so, in letters to other correspondents he – perhaps mischievously – countenanced the possibility that the Mecklenburg resolves were known to at least some delegates at the time. Jefferson, for his part, would have none of it. His reply to Adams continues: 'I deem it to be a very unjustifiable quiz ... It appeals to an original book, which is burnt, to Mr Alexander, who is dead, to a joint letter from Caswell, Hughes, and Hooper, all dead, to a copy sent to the dead Caswell, and another sent to Doctor Williamson, now probably dead, whose memory, now probably dead, did not recollect, in the history he has written of North Carolina, this gigantic step of its county of Mecklenburg ...' And then, in appealing to Adams's own, considerable, ego, he opines: 'Armed with this bold example, would not you have addressed our timid brethren in peals of thunder, on their tardy fears?' Furthermore, he writes, 'Would not every advocate of independence have rung the glories of Mecklenburg county in North Carolina in the ears of the doubting Dickinson and others, who hung so heavily on us?' 'Yet', he notes by way of hopefully sealing the fate of this scurrilous rumour, 'the example of independent Mecklenburg county, in North Carolina, was never once quoted.'

It seems very likely that Jefferson, the 'author of the Declaration of Independence', went to his grave convinced that the Mecklenburg resolves were a hoax. And many Jeffersonians took the same view. But the citizens of Charlotte, North Carolina, were not so easily persuaded. So, in 1830, the governor of the state, Montfort Stokes, set up a commission to inquire into the veracity of this story and to 'examine, collate, and arrange' all the documentary evidence that could be obtained. They faced one very significant problem: there was no written record extant of the meeting allegedly held through the night of 19 May 1775 and into the early hours of the morning of the 20th. The minutes taken at this meeting in Charlotte's courthouse, attended by twenty-six delegates, had been destroyed in a fire in April 1800 at the house of John McKnitt Alexander who had acted as secretary on the occasion. The members of the commission were aware of the claim that copies of these minutes had been made and sent to Hugh Williamson in New York who, at the time, had been writing a history of North Carolina. And that a further second set of the same notes were also supposed to have been sent to General W. R. Davie. None of these documents seemed to have survived.

Not to be disheartened by this lack of hard evidence they set about locating all those still alive who had played a part in the alleged activities. Once a surviving protagonist had been found they dispatched attorneys – some as far as Georgia – to take depositions from them. The number of survivors was not great. And they were, of course, by this time mostly aged men whose memories, at least according to some, were far from reliable. But all of those deposed corroborated the story that in May 1775 the citizens of Mecklenburg County resolved to separate from the mother country. It is true that the longest and perhaps most important deposition, given by the 88-year-old Captain Jack – the person instrumental in delivering the resolves to the delegates meeting in Philadelphia – has inconsistencies. He was, after all, well into his dotage. But the concluding text of his sworn testimony is completely unambiguous. It states that he 'delivered the Mecklenburg Declaration of Independence of May, 1775, to Richard Caswell and William Hooper, the Delegates to Congress from the State of North Carolina'.

Delivering their report in 1831, Governor Stokes's commission came to the same conclusion. The long report, complete with notarised depositions which to this day may be consulted, states that

> By the publication of these papers, it will be fully verified, that as early as the month of May, 1775, a portion of the people of North Carolina, sensible that their wrongs could no longer be borne, without sacrificing both safety and honor, and that redress so often sought, so patiently waited for, and so cruelly delayed, was no longer to be expected, did, by a public and solemn act, declare the dissolution of ties which bound them to the crown and people of Great Britain, and did establish an independent, though temporary government for their own control and direction.

If this is an accurate record of what transpired in Mecklenburg County during 1775 why did Caswell and Hooper fail to make much impression on their congressional colleagues?

According to one version of events they reported the resolves but, it is claimed, at that moment in 1775 the colonists were not ready to act in concert and go all the way with a declaration of independence. According to another version the delegates from North Carolina decided not to communicate the resolves taken by their compatriots in Charlotte because they believed them to be too inflammatory. Or, in another perhaps more credible hypothesis, given that such language and the intention expressed by it would have alerted the agents of the king to treasonable acts, Caswell and Hooper informally discussed these resolutions with colleagues and made sure that any open debate in Congress took place under the usual rules which placed an embargo on the taking of minutes or notes. And since there *are* no minutes of these meetings we will never know what happened to the intelligence Captain Jack delivered to the members of the Second Continental Congress. Or if he ever did deliver anything at all from the townsfolk of Mecklenburg County.

Historians of our own time have mostly been sceptical of this story, finding in it a series of contestable claims and shaky hypotheses. Most have concluded that the so-called resolves printed in the *Raleigh Register and North Carolina Gazette* must have been fabricated sometime long after the text of the Declaration had been agreed by the Second Continental Congress, and indeed far from providing the form of words for sections of that document it was precisely the other way round. The 'fake' Mecklenburg declaration simply copied the wording of the Philadelphia text. This argument, however, has a fatal flaw. If the so-called Mecklenburg resolves were taken from the Philadelphia Declaration the clause which appears in the allegedly fake document 'endowed by their creator with inherent and inalienable rights' ought to echo that in the officially adopted version of Congress. For, although Jefferson had written 'inherent and inalienable' in his draft, the final, printed version of the text has 'endowed by their creator with certain unalienable rights'. It has never been claimed, and indeed seems unlikely, that whoever wrote the 'fraudulent' Mecklenburg text had access to Jefferson's drafts.

Does any of this matter? If it is factually correct that the good citizens of Mecklenburg resolved to separate from Britain a year or so before the thirteen colonies acted in concert, what difference did this make to the course of history? Any more difference than the similar 'declarations' which were made in a number of colonies in the year or so before the Declaration was published? And how does this, albeit brief, piece of forensic historical analysis help us understand something about the force and power of the story of the Fourth? In order to answer those questions we need to look elsewhere, away from an incidental event in the history of the colonial period, for the real curiosity of this piece of local detail lies in the reaction of the third president upon hearing the news from his erstwhile colleague Adams. Why did Jefferson dismiss the story with such dispatch? Why did he protect his 'authorship' of the Declaration so vociferously? In doing so he was cultivating and protecting the narrative of the *punctual moment*. The story which claims that the colonies cut their ties to the mother country in a *single declaratory act*. As we have seen, although in retrospect it may have come to feel as if it had been like that to the actors in the drama playing throughout the summer of 1776 in Philadelphia, in point of fact, as their letters and journals indicate, at the time of its unfolding matters were rather more murky. Furthermore, in promoting this notion of the single declaratory act which led to the 'birth of the nation' another claim may also be entered: that an individual, or group of individuals, *made* that act. Call them the 'signers' or even the 'Founding Fathers'. Or, in the case of Thomas Jefferson, *the* author of the Declaration of Independence.

The significance that proprietorial rights were to assume over this act can be traced by focusing on the particular status accorded to the words which were adopted by the Second Continental Congress and subsequently published as the Declaration of Independence. For, as will become evident, the question of property rights in words was not a matter of indifference to those closely involved in the drafting of the document, prime amongst them Thomas Jefferson. One can begin by noting that title to the words in the document has been subject to variation over time. For those who literally made the declaration in July 1776, the delegates to the Second Continental Congress, the words were held as common property, within collective ownership, even if the delegates never, so far as we know, formally 'made' the declaration in the sense of speaking out loud the words of the text they had finally agreed to.

This was for a very good reason: the words of the document printed on instruction from the Congress and issued on 4 July performed a very specific task. They were to indict the monarch on a large number of counts of negligence and improper action. These, the colonists held, were proof of the fact that George III had abdicated his role as sovereign. This is why the document has the air and formality of a legal writ. In drafting the text the delegates – nearly half of whom were practising lawyers – very clearly had in mind legal precedents for their case but they were far from secure in regard to the protection the prevailing law might have offered them.

Consequently no single person, at the time of its making, would have even felt it appropriate, still less comfortable, to claim for himself ownership of the words which comprise the document. For we must remember that at the time of its being made public those words provided ample cause for a charge of treason to be levied on whosoever declared them. It was not merely the practical advantage of combining resources which motivated the colonists to seeking unanimity over the issue of separation. Strength in numbers was seen as one of the few protective measures within their reach – something they learnt from both the history books and legal treatises which were their guides in constitutional matters.

But once separation from the mother country had been effected, once Washington had begun his campaign to successfully defend and protect the colonies from their oppressors, the document's significance and meaning altered. Then, once the new nation had been fully established, the moment at which Congress had publicly declared its independence from British oppression began to take on the trappings of an heroic act, performed by the courageous men who were to become the nation's Founding Fathers. It might be said that rivalry and amour-propre were no strangers to this constellation of strong-willed and in many cases visionary revolutionaries. Within this later context the Declaration began to be understood not as *a* significant document but as *the* founding act of the new republic. And here rivalry began to become apparent – all the more so since the two beasts in this particular jungle, the second and third presidents, were to end up on opposing sides of the emerging party political structure of the now United States of America. There was, then, considerable political capital to be made out of the claim that one had 'authored' the text of the nation's founding.

So let us return to Jefferson's reply to the letter of 19 July 1819 that he received from his then reconciled revolutionary colleague, John Adams. Does this now look like a case of special pleading? Was he really unaware of the Mecklenburg resolves? Here, once again, is the third of the 22 May Mecklenburg resolves, which states:

> That we do hereby declare ourselves a free and independent people; are, and of right ought to be, a sovereign and self-governing Association, under the control of no power other than that of our God and the general government of the Congress; to the maintenance of which independence, we solemnly pledge to each other our mutual co-operation, our lives, our fortunes, and our most sacred honor.

If we read this sentence alongside the last paragraph of the 4 July Declaration the similarity in phrasing and diction is so close that one must wonder whether Caswell and Hooper did in fact give some airing to the document delivered to them by Captain Jack. Here is the later text:

> That these United Colonies are, and of right ought to be Free and Independent States; that they are absolved from all allegiance to the British Crown, and that all political connection between them and the State of Great Britain is and ought to be totally dissolved; and that as Free and Independent States they have full power to levy war, conclude peace, contract alliances, establish commerce, and to do all other acts and things which independent

States may of right do. And for the support of this declaration, with a firm reliance on the protection of Divine Providence, we mutually pledge to each other our lives, our fortunes and our sacred honor.

Late in life Jefferson was both too grand and too fêted for the charge of plagiarism to stick, but he did, nevertheless, commit himself to paper on this issue in such a way as to leave the door open as to whether or not 'his' words were really his. Writing to Henry Lee on 8 May 1825 he admitted that, 'When forced, therefore, to resort to arms for redress, an appeal to the tribunal of the world was deemed proper for our justification. This was the object of the Declaration of Independence.' It was not, he said, 'to find out new principles, or new arguments, never before thought of, not merely to say things which had never been said before; but to place before mankind the common sense of the subject, in terms so plain and firm as to command their assent, and to justify ourselves in the independent stand we are compelled to take.' In other words he saw himself more as a conduit or mouthpiece for the general views all round him in Philadelphia than as the author of a document which would bear his own name.

In words which have become renowned he continues to explain to Lee how he understood his commission from the Congress: 'Neither aiming at originality of principle or sentiment', he continues, 'nor yet copied from any particular and previous writing, it was intended to be an expression of the American mind, and to give to that expression the proper tone and spirit called for by the occasion.' In the extensive literature on this extraordinary architect of the nation the success of Jefferson's endeavours in this regard is, quite rightly, repeatedly emphasised and the brilliance with which he managed to convey 'the American mind' often remarked upon. There's no sense that the third president 'owned' the words of the Declaration, or that only he was equipped to make a claim of this kind. Indeed Jefferson himself made the point in his letter to Lee that 'All its [the declaration's] authority rests then on the harmonizing sentiments of the day, whether expressed in conversation, in letters, printed essays, or in the elementary books of public right, as Aristotle, Cicero, Locke, Sidney, &.' Furthermore, as we know from the exhaustive work that has uncovered the archaeological texture of the document, the accepted revisions made by Congress to Jefferson's draft meant that words he had never even penned made it into the final document. And we also know that even if the Mecklenburg resolves never came to light in Philadelphia that summer, even if they are in fact fictitious, there are other examples of resolutions adopted around the colonies in the period leading up to the declaration on 4 July in which similar or even identical phrases are used. The Ulster–Scottish community of Palmer, Massachusetts, for example, sent word on 17 June to Congress that they supported a move for separation. Their resolve closed: 'we do unanimously determine and declare we will support them with our lives and fortunes'. This only strengthens Jefferson's admission that he saw his main task as harmonising 'the sentiments of the day'.

It is all the more strange, then, that Jefferson allowed, even encouraged, the idea to be put about that he was 'the statesman who drew the memorable Declaration of Independence', as democratic-republicans called him in the early nineteenth century in their toasts to the Fourth. And as he honed and refined the self-image that he wished to give to posterity he became increasingly in thrall to the myth that *the* founding document had *a singular* origin. And so he fabricated the person who would be known to history from the words he wrote down in 1826 intended to convey his life's accomplishments. Words he deemed appropriate for his tombstone. They read:

Here was buried
Thomas Jefferson
Author of the Declaration of American Independence
Of the Statute of Virginia for religious freedom
& Father of the University of Virginia

This identification with the 'author' of the Declaration became so complete, so compelling, that he was able to forget that in at least one conspicuous detail he had never been the author of *all* the words of that now famous document. He had never even *copied* these words into his drafts of the document that Congress was to debate. For the phrase in the last paragraph of the document that reads 'that these united colonies are and of right ought to be free and independent states', words which echo the Mecklenburg resolves, were adopted by Congress in place of Jefferson's rather more pointed 'reject and renounce all allegiance and subjection to the kings of Great Britain'. And Congress was using its own earlier 7 June resolution in which these words appear, words which had been penned by another Virginian, Richard Henry Lee. Since Jefferson was far from comfortable with the process by which the Committee of the Whole amended and altered his original draft it must have taken an act of extreme will to forget that one of the most resounding phrases of the document's last paragraph had been borrowed from his Virginian compatriot's motion of 7 June.

It is easy enough to grant to Jefferson the fiction that he had 'authored' the text that is now celebrated, for his accomplishments were indeed on a superhuman scale. We are happy to buy into this small departure from the facts because it corresponds with what we believe at the level of self-evident truth. Someone went off and drafted the document that would subsequently be revised, and that person was incontestably Thomas Jefferson. Even if *all* the words of the final text were not his – and in what sense are words one's own property in any case? – it hardly matters since they convey a set of aspirations and ideals we continue to subscribe to. But, more importantly for the argument of this book, allowing that the Declaration of Independence has *an* author contains the same architecture of belief as the proposition that America has *a* birthday: 4 July.

The following chapters set out to show how that architecture was established and maintained. And, in coming to understand that, it is to be hoped that the chances of building noble and enduring edifices with it will be improved.

2

MAKING INDEPENDENCE DAY

The first anniversary of the Fourth fell on a Friday. No one – at least no one in the Second Continental Congress – had given much thought to the notion that something might be done to mark the occasion, precisely a year earlier, when the intention to separate from the mother country had become public. This ought not to surprise us since the future of the colonies – still at war in early July 1777 – was at the time very uncertain. Although some of the delegates to Congress may have predicted an outcome which effectively sealed the fate of a new confederation of states there was still much discussion and debate ahead on matters of great significance – on the constitution of what would become a single republic, the relations between its constituent states and the nature of government itself in a republican confederation. Put simply, there was not much – yet – to celebrate.

Nevertheless on Wednesday 2 July 1777 Congress turned its collective attention to the matter of what, if anything, ought to be done in Philadelphia on Friday the 4th. As with so many of its decisions nothing was agreed then and there, postponing until the following day the discussion at which it was proposed and agreed that on the 4th, Congress would adjourn for the day. Most, if not all of the delegates were in favour of asking someone to give a sermon but it was too late to organise this for the following day. Instead it was agreed that the delegates would have dinner together.

As it turned out, rather more noise was made that day than might occur at a simple repast. John Adams wrote to his daughter on 5 July that he had gone on board a frigate, the *Delaware*, accompanied by the president of the council and 'several gentlemen of the Marine Committee'. A salute of thirteen guns was fired off followed by a response from thirteen further ships in the river. Adams, who was rather boosterish about the matter of celebrating the separation, recounts: 'The wharves and shores were lined with a vast concourse of people, all shouting and hurrahing in a manner which gave great joy to every friend to this country and the utmost terror and dismay to every lurking tory.'

This reference to 'lurking tories' reminds us that one year on, in 1777, there were still serious voices of dissent to be heard in the colonies over the matter of the 'rebellion', as His Majesty referred to the War of Independence that was ongoing at the time. And indeed for the following thirty years the Fourth was marked by a severe division in party and political allegiance all over the former colonies. Far from celebrating the founding of the nation, the Fourth – at least in the immediate years following the declaration – provided a locale and occasion for the continuing battle over the *history and future* of the confederation. Over its allegiance to a past that tied it to the mother country and a future that might or might not seek to reconfigure that relation as one of economic and diplomatic dependence. And it is this – the sense of facing both the past and the future – which provides the *structure* of the ritual of observance embedded in the Fourth to this day. For as long as the republic endures it is, above all else, this *structural* configuration of the rites of observance for the Fourth that will enable the nation simultaneously to both commemorate and instantiate, as if for the first time, its origin. It is this which makes America's signature legible: poised between a commemorative right that is widely understood to honour the *signing* of the Declaration and an enactment of independence in the vocal declaration of the words Congress published to the world. A signature whose form is the belief that the many speak as one.

Adams may well have embellished his account of the festivities in Philadelphia on that first anniversary just a little since he, like Jefferson, was committed to the fiction of a punctual moment for the origin of the nation. But even if he did, his account was to prove prescient in the longer term, at least, since 'bonfires in the streets and fireworks' were to become defining features of celebrations on the Fourth. In the immediate aftermath of the declaration, however, more pressing and local political priorities were uppermost in the minds of celebrants. Even so, before the second anniversary rolled around, Congress determined that the Fourth would, henceforth, be honoured with a 'public celebration of the anniversary of independence at Philadelphia' in a vote of 24 June 1778.

The fate of the Fourth as a nationally respected day of commemoration and celebration was not yet sealed; in fact it was not until 1870 that federal legislation was passed making the day into an official national holiday. Nevertheless local customs were already being codified into legislation from the early 1780s. Massachusetts was first to enshrine the celebration as an official event in the yearly calendar in a resolve asking the governor to 'direct that suitable preparation be made for the celebration of the Anniversary of the United States of America'. This formulation of the focus of the celebrations was to prove to be deeply satisfying and, in time, almost universally adopted. In this regard Massachusetts was a trail-blazer: the drift towards national acceptance of the purpose and utility of a day devoted to the celebration of 'the Anniversary of the United States' was mired in the long struggle over the precise nature of the political bonds of the Union and the role that federal government was to play in the delicate set of relations between the constituent parts of the new nation.

Notwithstanding the long process of national adoption, the vote passed by Congress on 24 June 1778 did determine a second extremely important feature of the character of celebration that to this day persists in the honouring of the Fourth. The vote reads: 'Resolved that Congress will, in a body, attend divine worship on Sunday, the 5th day of July next, to return thanks for the divine mercy in supporting the independence of these States and that the chaplains be requested to officiate and to preach sermons suited to the occasion.' Although these two moments of observance – the public celebration of the Fourth and the collective attendance at church the following day – were distinct in 1778, they became almost instantaneously fused together. For what characterises the structure of celebration for the anniversary of the declaration from 1778 and thereafter is a strange hybridisation of the public and private, the political and the devotional: a kind of sacralisation of the political.

All over the emerging new republic the predominant feature of the celebration which could be said to contain a manifest content was an oration. In most cases this was given by a preacher from the community but important townsfolk – the mayor or a well-known attorney – also had their turn. And these orations, at least in the first half-century following independence, took a shared template that was supposed to recall and invoke those beliefs which had led to the separation of the colonies from the mother country. In particular the orator was to consider the feelings, manners and principles appropriate to the occasion and to move through five topics. The first was the causes of the revolution, the second the 'distinguished characters' who played a role in the event, followed by an explicit recognition of the role France played in bringing a successful conclusion to the process of independence. The fourth topic, the 'superior advantages' of a republican government, no doubt played differently to politically partisan audiences, while the fifth, the supreme importance of public and private virtue, was less contentious (even if its basis in a particular version of republican ideology may have also been rebarbative to some).

Orations were not the only common feature of the celebrations. Other rites, less obviously connected to the fusion of church and state but still very much enacting a bridge between the public and private, were also quickly established. Dinners, for example, were almost universally adopted as a way of bringing people together in celebration, although the timing of these meals was determined by local climate – July in the southern states was not conducive to open-air feasts at almost any time of the day or night. And dinners were frequently punctuated by toasts. From the very first celebrations, fireworks or the firing of cannon or muskets, were a feature of the day, as were military parades of one sort or another. Both can, of course, be read as political acts or as participating in the domain of political representation.

These two sentiments contained in the 24 June vote of Congress in 1778 – on the one hand the directive to hold a public celebration and on the other the resolution to gather

together in divine worship – provide the germ for all subsequent 4 July celebrations. One might say that the hinge
which articulates these two distinct features of the Fourth,
the public manifestation of belonging to a common cause
and the private observance of faith, provides the very genetic
imprint for this new body politic, the first modern republic.
Which is not to say that the celebratory practices of 4 July
comprise a singular politics. Far from it, as the history of the
first fifty or so years demonstrates. But what may well turn
out to be the most impressive and enduring strength of this
combination of the devotional and the secular celebration is
its elasticity. Adaptation and inclusion are seamlessly woven
into the traditions of the Fourth which has enabled many
different constituencies to speak in the language of origins
and with the rhetoric of authenticity. One, the individual
about his or her private devotions, is gathered up into the
heterodox celebrations of the many.

What I mean by this hinge can be understood from the
discussions in Congress around the third anniversary. In 1779
the 4th fell on a Sunday, and this caused some consternation
in a constituency which, although not entirely comprised of
devout Protestants, many of whom belonged to what today
would be called 'low church' congregations, nevertheless
recognised the Sabbath as not only culturally or devotion-
ally significant but also politically so. Consequently, following a discussion which had divided the delegates, a vote was
passed seven to three – New Hampshire, Connecticut and
New Jersey voting against – 'that the Chaplain of Congress
be requested to prepare a sermon suitable to the occasion'
and this was to be the only mark of observance of the anniversary on that day, Sunday the 4th. But then 'a further
motion was made that the President cause an entertainment

to be prepared on the 5th of July in celebration of the independence of these United States'. And since that day every year in which the Fourth falls on a Sunday celebration of Independence Day in most places around the country has been postponed to Monday the 5th (although some towns have opted to go a day earlier, on Saturday the 3rd).

Once again the hinge between the private devotional and the public celebratory is revealed in descriptions of the Fourth as the 'Sabbath of our Freedom', an expression used by the *Independent Gazetteer*, on 11 July 1789, or 'a sabbath in the calendar of liberty' by another local newspaper of the time. One can also see it in the quickly established form of the oration on the Fourth which was in effect a secular version of the Sabbath day service and often held in church buildings. During the early nineteenth century there was no embarrassment in openly referring to the Fourth in religious terms. A Boston newspaper of 1810, the *Columbian Centinel*, remarked of that year's celebrations in the city as having proceeded with 'more religious rites and with greater festive pomp than for many years past'. And by the jubilee in 1826 the orator for the occasion in Boston, Mayor Josiah Quincy, described the observance of the rituals of the Fourth as 'a solemn and somewhat religious duty'. Such overt religiosity casts a long shadow that is still perceivable in many contemporary versions of the American Project even if for many the practices of everyday life are resolutely secular. Here once more we can see the strength of a hinge: it allows for both secular and devotional forms of commemoration.

Although the first ten or so years following 1776 saw mainly local traditions being established, some of which were focused on events specific to the region such as the Boston Massacre of 5 March 1770, the general trend was to give way to the significance of the Fourth. Indeed, as we have seen above, the first 'official' state recognition of the 4th as a day of celebration, referring to the festivities held in Massachusetts in 1781, introduced one form for the phrase – 'the Anniversary of the United States of America' – which right to the present time encapsulates the 'meaning' or purpose of the day. And in that gesture of origination it was almost as if the prehistory of the nation, the history of colonial dependence, was to be erased. The birth of this new entity brought into the world a new polis comprising citizens each and every one of whom embodied a set of virtues that defined the future for the new republic, and expressed their consent to be governed in their willing inclusion in the 'we' who spoke for it. Those virtues can be gathered together and symbolically represented in one word: independence.

This word was, of course, in the years immediately following the Declaration, freighted with political meanings articulating the desire to gain and maintain freedom from what had previously been seen to keep the colonists in bondage. Where His Majesty sought to maintain their subservience and bind them to the corruptions of colonial rule, Americans now claimed rights and freedoms that belonged to them *in their own right*. Independence, to the generation of '76, was a virtue on behalf of the fact of being a citizen. But to later generations the capacity of the term to attract and hold within itself more capacious and circumstantial meanings – ethical as well as political – allowed it to become associated with the myth of origin that was so firmly promoted by those early celebrants who feared for the continuation of the new republic and strenuously sought to create an identity for it. Independence, to these men and women, was not only a political fact. It was at the core of a new kind of person, a citizen claiming universal rights. And the birth of the nation is the crucible within which this new citizen comes into being. It is a story of biblical proportions in which virtue, freedom and independence are fused together in a new dawn that almost has the capacity to rewrite the fall from grace undergone in the garden of Eden.

We can detect the biblical rhetoric which pushes celebration of the Fourth in this direction from the wording of the 1783 resolution passed in Boston. This vote states that the city resolved to honour the 'Fourth of July, A.D. 1776' as a day 'ever memorable in the Annals of this country for the Declaration of our Independence' and it went on to prescribe the nature of the observance stipulated for celebrations from that time forward. Each year on 4 July, for ever more, there was to be a 'Publick Oration' delivered in a location deemed proper by the town officials. And in the course of this speech 'the Orator shall consider the feelings, manners and principles which led to this great National Event as well as the important and happy effects whether general or domestick which already have and will forever continue to flow from the Auspicious Epoch'. Although this directive was specific to Bostonians it nevertheless captures the form of countless Independence Day orations all over the new nation. Even so, the content of such speeches was not immune to political contingencies, so by 1788 when the country was locked into battle over the adoption of a federal constitution the Fourth and its traditions of celebration were marshalled into a party political conflict that was to endure for a number of years.

Prior to this internecine battle around the final decade of the century – in the years immediately following the Declaration – the meanings of the Fourth were closely tied to the requirement to maintain morale in the face of an uncertain future. The longevity of the new republic was at that time still to be determined. Consequently any celebrations that took place on the Fourth were coloured by the necessities of war and the need to keep morale high. This explains the frequent exposition of the 'spirit of '76' and the almost obsessive reiteration of the virtues of the founders (albeit inflected by party political loyalties) and of republicanism in general. And the same impetus gave rise to the sense that it was crucial to re-imagine, even re-experience, the state of bondage which had been the immediate cause of the revolution. These inflections of the rituals of the Fourth played a vital part in the process of founding a new identity since it was a matter of survival for the nation that its citizens continued to hold a vivid picture of the war in their heads, and that they *felt* the honourable gift of the lives of those citizens who had perished at the hands of the oppressors. While veterans of the war were still living, this sense of linking the present of remembrance each Fourth of July to the *real* of the revolution was a significant feature of the celebratory practices observed on the day. And although the last few veterans lived beyond the jubilee the fact that two of the principal architects of the new nation died within hours of each other on that day, 4 July 1826, was widely taken to signal a new phase in the practice and meanings of celebration.

Intervening between then and the end of the War of Independence we find a different set of partisan political interests asserting themselves around the observance of the Fourth. From the late 1780s what one did and said on the Fourth became a hot potato. In the years of heated discussion leading to the Philadelphia Convention of 1787 which was to thrash out the Constitution two factions had emerged.

On the one hand 'federalists' supported Madison's scheme which gave significant powers to a federal government while on the other 'anti-federalists', who later became known as 'democratic-republicans', vainly fought for the maintenance of the pre-eminent power of state legislatures. Many of the provisions of Madison's Constitution sought to bring the individual states into a collective political entity which had the power to direct and drive the country forward through the interlocking institutions of the bicameral federal legislature and the offices of state, most especially that of the president. Those who wished to preserve what they saw as the indispensable architecture of a true republic and the principles upon which the revolution had been based, namely the autonomy of its constituent parts, each state's legislature, opposed the moves towards Madison's blueprint for the new nation. As far as the anti-federalists were concerned he was merely proposing to reinstitute the monarch under a different guise.

These opposing political groups in the now firmly established republic sought to reclaim independence for their own specific party political purposes. Republicanism now had another set of meanings, resonating with another struggle that erupted in Europe at the century's end. This, within the context of the fierce battle that had been entered into over the precise terms and structure of a federal constitution, led to a deeply divisive view about the recent past and the future direction for the infant new nation. If the years immediately following the Declaration in '76 had managed to instil a sense of common purpose – had in effect created a common past for the citizens who came into being with the declarative act itself – the years following the adoption of the Constitution witnessed a bifurcation of allegiance and the promotion of a contested collection of identifications. Now, it appeared, there were contrasting views about what the revolution had been about, what it had been for, and whether or not it had ended.

Federalists abhorred the events in France and saw their opponents, the 'anti-federalists', as promoting a set of values that were inimical to the purposes of the revolution and that would, if adopted, lead to nothing less than the destruction of what they considered to be the American republican experiment. From the other side, anti-federalists saw their opponents as nothing more than rebranded monarchists. And each side in this partisan political struggle sought to claim the Fourth for its own purposes.

In some cities, such as Boston, the fight between opposing ideologies was brought to an indelicate climax each Fourth of July. Federalists and anti-federalists each met in their own locations and co-opted the symbols of the day – the flag, orations, the liberty cap and so forth – for their own ends. Militia from each side paraded through particular parts of the city and dinners became the occasion for expressing loyalty to a specific party cause. To make matters more fraught the Society of the Cincinnati, comprised of almost exclusively federalist supporters, chose the Fourth for the date of their annual meeting and dinner, thereby exacerbating the intense rivalry that surrounded the battle for the future of the nation. Furthermore, the federalists, at least in Boston and Philadelphia, almost held a monopoly over the rites which characterised the celebrations. The official orators chosen to speak were almost always federalist, and the toasts at the dinners were almost exclusively designed to ennoble federalist heroes of the cause – Washington, Hancock, John and Samuel Adams. The record indicates that for forty years following the Declaration the name of Jefferson was not uttered in a formal toast at any federalist dinner in Boston. Perhaps this should not surprise us since anti-federalists were equally inattentive to Jefferson's role in drafting the Declaration until he became vice-president in 1797.

The following year a Boston anti-federalist newspaper was referring to the 'immortal Jefferson', which only served to highlight the deep divisions that now ran through party politics. Bostonians began to feel the wounds very keenly so that by the Fourth of July 1799 the *Independent Chronicle* was counselling the suspension of hostilities, urging that 'we lay aside the divisions which disgrace us when the glory of our country calls us to unite in the celebration of her honour and independence ... Let the spirit of 1776 prevent us, when established as a sovereign power, from crumbling into parties.' But that same year federalist celebrants in Philadelphia continued to toast their heroes Washington and Adams and to neglect Jefferson. In riposte their opponents toasted Vice-President Jefferson as the 'statesman who drew the memorable Declaration of Independence – may his virtue and patriotism live forever in the hearts of the freemen of America', and from this time on, the indissoluble association of Jefferson's name with the text of the Declaration began to gain ground.

As Jefferson's stock began to rise in the third presidential race those who continued to oppose his election began to find ways of criticising what had by now become the traditional forms for celebrating the Fourth. Where until now the general festivities and commotion – firing off muskets, fireworks, parades and so forth – had been indulged in by both sides in the political firmament these practices began to become targets for those who wished to minimise any association between the recently constituted republic and revolutionary fervour across the Atlantic. The link between the American and French revolutions had been an element in 'democratic' anti-federal celebrations from the early 1790s. The Democratic Society of Philadelphia, for example, held its first Fourth celebration in 1794, to which it invited 'other patriotic citizens', and its supporters also celebrated ten days later, on the 14th, to mark the occasion of the fall of the Bastille. Such open embrace of what, to some, were dangerous – even anarchic – political beliefs and sympathies ran the risk of corrupting the orderly development of the United States and of dangerously making common cause with revolutionaries around the world. This was a sentiment that anti-federalist republicans in Boston, for example, abhorred, and they lost little time in showing it by flying the French and Dutch flags alongside the colours of the United States on Independence Day in 1796.

A similar motivation prompted 'democratic-republicans' in Philadelphia to fly the American and French flags joined together at the top under a French liberty cap which had been augmented with an American cockade. These and other 'inflammatory' interpretations of the rituals and symbols of the Fourth prompted a Philadelphia newspaper to note that: 'It is said that some Federalists begin to think that the celebration of the 4th of July is not a matter of most importance, that it frequently creates riot and disturbance and that it would be more productive of good order to discontinue in future any particular attachment to the Anniversary.' And, perhaps unsurprisingly, the tone of reproach very quickly began to sound moralising. Good citizens, those who supported the federal cause, would not condone the riotous behaviour or loose talk which characterised the dinners held on the Fourth by anti-federalists, who were by now commonly known as 'democrats'. According to them the toasts proposed were 'seditious and treasonable and flagrantly immoral and flagitious', as the Philadelphian *Gazette of the United States* of 14 July 1800 put it. Moreover, if the 'sentiments exhibited in the drunken revels of democrats were realized and acted upon, the State would topple headlong and all the bands of morality would be unloosed'.

During these last years of the century, party political skirmishes aside, the gradual acceptance of the Fourth as a national holiday to be substantially spent away from the workplace became widespread. Even so, in 1793 a French visitor to Philadelphia could still note that, while the celebrations on the Fourth were marked by the ringing of church bells and the firing of cannon, nevertheless 'more than three fourths of the stores remain open'. A year later the *Gazette of the United States* asked its readers, especially those who had the power to act, to 'let the hand of industry be suspended'. And so it became. Banks began to close, turning the day into a bank holiday. By 1802 in Philadelphia virtually all business was suspended for the day and observing the anniversary was deemed to be a correct way of demonstrating one's patriotism – no matter which party one supported. This pattern was echoed across the country and as momentum for a public holiday gained ground the nature of the celebration began to evolve.

In the years immediately following 1776, whether or not the Fourth was observed as a punctual moment in the short history of the nation, the future still seemed inextricably tied to the act of declaration. And while the principal players in the Second Continental Congress were still alive the *commemorative* function of observance on the day was likely to be uppermost in the minds of celebrants wherever they were located. But inevitably, as the generation of '76 died, the ties to Philadelphia's State House and the act of declaration began to loosen. Anti-federalists in the 1790s remade those ties in a very striking fashion – they started the tradition of reading the Declaration each Fourth. And since they were committed to supporting the person who now became widely known as the 'author' of that document, anything that revived the true *republican* spirit of '76 was grist to the mill of their partisan politics. For the same reasons for fifteen years in the early nineteenth century Boston's *Independent Chronicle* reprinted the text of the Declaration on its front page every 4 July.

But alongside these politically opportunistic uses of the Fourth there also developed a more open-ended sense of how the celebrations of the day might be adapted and enlisted in projects of a very varied kind. In fact the party political uses of the celebration throughout the 1790s helped to create a feeling for the plasticity of the day's significations. Civic projects of different sorts suddenly became 'sanctified' by their being tied to Fourth celebrations. In 1795, for example, the foundation stone of Massachusetts' new State House in Boston was laid by two heroes of the revolution, Samuel Adams and Paul Revere. In 1818 the same city officially began the building of its General Hospital on Independence Day. If one wanted to launch a new initiative – say a contest to find a new national patriotic song, as the Philadelphia Military Association did – then the Fourth was the day to do it. And so to this day all manner of events have been bundled into the extraordinarily capacious maw of the Fourth of July – the laying of a railroad, opening a civic institution, the construction of a canal, the dedication of a monument, the naturalization of immigrants, the defeat of tyrants. It is this openness, the symbolic generosity of the Fourth which gives it such potency and longevity. The genius of the formulation in the Declaration – not to diminish the Herculean labours of the great artificer of the Constitution, Madison – lies in precisely its openness. For what is held to be self-evident truth is not prescribed: it states that 'among these truths …'. Herein lies America's magnificent power of self fashioning.

By the time of the jubilee in 1826 most aspects of the public celebrations which were not tied to specific local traditions had hardened into an institution. Although not all of these elements persist unchanged, many remain recognisable even if our daily lives are significantly altered in shape from those of citizens of the late eighteenth century. First up is the ringing of bells and the firing of cannon. The latter may no longer be common but modern equivalents have certainly played and continue to play their role. In the early days the bells would ring for half an hour following sunrise on the Fourth and then again at noon and sunset. The most obvious near connection to this practice was muster day or certain church occasions.

Second up was the military parade. Again in the early days the local militia paraded through the town or city, watched by the children and wives of the menfolk who served as the protectors of the municipality. This practice seamlessly evolved into the military parade of the armed forces familiar from more recent experience. Following the militiamen in the parade came functionaries such as the governor, mayor, members of the Society of the Cincinnati or simply the resident men of power or distinction. The destination was usually a large civic building or space, failing that, a church. The parade almost always ended with a fired salute – the number of shots growing as the Union itself grew.

Once inside the building or standing in a town square the order of observance was most obviously modelled on that of a Protestant church service. A clergyman might initiate proceedings with a prayer, to be followed by a patriotic song and then the reading of a poem or some patriotic text, frequently penned for the occasion by a local writer. Towards the final years of the century the Declaration was invariably read in republican-leaning observance and into the nineteenth century this became a feature of almost all celebrations. By 1825, the year of Lafayette's celebratory tour around the country, the Frenchman who held honorary status as one of the revolutionary generation noted that the custom of reading the Declaration aloud had spread into the home itself. Having listened to this part of the ritual, ears were pricked up for the real heart of the matter: the oration by a minister or municipal functionary.

Following the oration the company made its way to another location – most commonly a large square or green out of doors, but where a hall large enough existed it might be inside – for a communal but exclusively masculine dinner. Dignitaries were placed around the tables and the food was often prepared by a local tavern keeper. Although there is no enduring tradition of food served from the eighteenth century to today – Independence Day does not retain a significant role for the equivalent of, say, a Thanksgiving turkey – nevertheless at different times and in particular regions traditions did emerge. In the early years the most widely adopted was the consumption of turtle soup and ice cream. No matter what food was served, copious quantities of refreshment were provided, including beer, cider and spirits. A second oration at the dinner might be given but the

universal activity which accompanied eating was the proposal of toasts.

The practice of toasting was deeply embedded in eight-
eenth-century British culture. Almost any occasion, public
or familial, might provide an opportunity to raise a glass
to the monarch or some auspicious figure, dead or alive. In
colonial America this practice was continued but unsurprisingly toasting the king or mother country became increasingly fraught around the time of the Stamp Act and its
subsequent reverberations. Immediately after the revolution the first toast, which by British tradition was always to
the monarch, became replaced by one to 'the Nation'. The
number of toasts proposed on the Fourth was symbolically
tied to the commemorative function of the day: thirteen, for
the thirteen colonies which had signed the Declaration. But
frequently, as spirits became more lively, those attending
the meal were moved to propose further toasts, most often
as a way of indicating agreement with a particular regional
issue or allegiance to a local cause or person. Even the 'official' toasts – to the heroes of '76, say – were subject to the
vagaries of party political pressures. As the nation settled
into its mature identity the toasts became less partisan in
tone and sympathy, but they never lost their capacity to
respond to immediate concerns and regional identities, a
feature that persists in current celebrations of the day. One
can get a sense of the flavour of these encomia from some
examples, such as that of the celebrants in Georgia who in
1789 proposed a toast to 'the principle of patriotism, and the
spirit of union, to pervade the states of North Carolina and
Rhode Island' in the hope of encouraging those two states
to ratify the Constitution. More barbed was the toast proposed by federalists in Springfield, Massachusetts, in 1808

while Jefferson was entering the last year of his presidency. These disgruntled folk proposed a toast to 'The President of the United States – to ruin a country, govern it by a French Philosopher – we hail the fourth of March 1809', the date upon which a new president was to be inaugurated. But even taking account of local incidental loyalties or enthusiasms the conformity of the sequence of toasts across the country by 1826 was quite remarkable. What by then had become the initial toast 'to the Day' or 'the ever memorable 4th July, 1776' was almost universally respected. As was the second, to the 'patriots and sages' or the 'departed heroes'. The name of Washington seems to have been usually attached to this toast or to the third which was either to 'the president of the United States' or to 'the Constitution of the United States'. From here onwards more narrowly defined custom and political allegiance began to assert themselves, as toasts to a state figure or proximate militia company might be proposed and so on down to the symbolically resonant thirteenth.

If these activities provide the core of the structure of celebration for the Fourth a very wide range of additional entertainments could be indulged in. At various times in the history of the Fourth between 1777 and today these have included theatrical performances, concerts, hot-air ballooning, horse racing, parades dedicated to many different causes, and increasingly in more recent times demonstrations mounted by those disaffected with some aspect of contemporary American life and politics. But whatever inflection might be given to the day its conclusion has been, at least in aspiration, unwavering and almost universally applauded: fireworks.

Alas – to many aficionados of the entertainment – pyro-

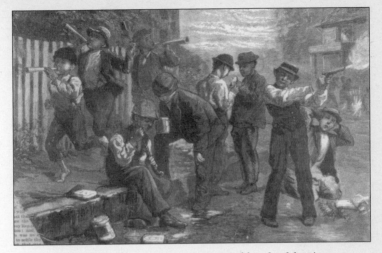

3. A late-nineteenth century depiction of fourth celebrations.

technic displays have also had their ups and downs. In the early twentieth century a campaign to make the day's events 'safe and sane' led to the attempt to restrict the sale of fireworks since the casualty rate from improperly ignited or carelessly aimed rockets and crackers had been deemed to be unacceptable. As the above print from 1878 shows (illustration 3), boys having fun with horns may be one thing, firing pistols another. A century earlier, in 1778 and indeed in the war years following the Declaration, gunpowder was a valuable commodity whose use was directed at more pressing matters. Nevertheless, the first celebrations included 'illuminations' – usually candles set up in windows and in public places. Given the absence of street lighting such illuminated scenes often struck contemporary observers with delight and amazement. But candles are nowhere near as exciting as the thunderclap and sparkle of fireworks. Once they became relatively inexpensive and widely available no

Fourth celebration was complete without a firework display, no matter how modest. And some, like the mock re-creation of an atomic bomb exploding in the harbour at Baltimore in 1951, must have been truly mind-blowing.

FREEDOM'S JUBILEE

By the 1820s the intense partisan political rivalry of the early decades of the century had become less pronounced and observance of the Fourth's rites slowly began to be more inclusive. Women, for example, began to take a full part in the celebrations, organising their own versions of the by-now standard elements of the day. Where the menfolk con-tinued to hold their drink-fuelled suppers, women gathered together at tea parties, or, like the 'Sabbath School Unions' formed in New England, gathered for picnics that day. Dancing and socialising as the evening wore on became a socially mixed affair and diversions for children began to comprise an increasingly large part of the celebrations. As 1826 loomed on the horizon thoughts turned to the fifti-eth anniversary of the Declaration and once again the pro-claimed punctuality of the historical event began to exert its considerable powers of bewitchment. Interest in the early years of the nation had intensified as the decade of the 1820s arrived, perhaps nowhere more tellingly indicated than by the popularity of the nine-volume *Biography of the Signers of the Declaration of Independence* which Joseph Sanderson began to publish in 1823 (and only completed the year fol-lowing the jubilee). Amazingly, by the turn of 1826 three of its subjects were still alive: John Adams, at ninety-one years, was living in his family home at Quincy. Charles Carroll of Carrollton, one of the signatories to the Declaration from

Maryland, was eighty-nine. And Thomas Jefferson, though in poor health at eighty-three, was still occasionally receiving visitors at Monticello.

Congress appointed thirteen members to its Committee of Arrangements and charged it with the responsibility of organising the Capitol's golden-jubilee celebrations. Their first thought was to invite all the living signers of the Declaration along with all surviving former presidents to Washington for the festivities. It turned out that none of these men of '76 was able to attend but they all sent elegant letters of regret which were reprinted in the newspapers. Jefferson, as one might expect, though close to his final weeks wrote in terms which encapsulate the enduring quality of the Fourth: its combination of the retrospective, commemorative preservation of the past with the prospective pledge of allegiance to a future always yet-to-come. His letter is worth citing at length since it conveys so well the intricately wound strands of the fabric of Jefferson's self-fashioning, his sense of his own role in the founding of the nation and of the nation's role in the promotion of a universal brotherhood of man. He wrote:

Respected Sir:
The kind invitation I received from you, on the part of the citizens of the city of Washington, to be present with them at their celebration of the Fiftieth Anniversary of American Independence, as one of the surviving signers of an instrument, pregnant with our own and with the fate of the world, is most flattering to myself ...

There is Jefferson's always coyly gauche self-aggrandisement: 'is most flattering to myself'. It occurs as if by surprise to the writer himself and comes embedded in the deftly pointed albeit understated political rallying call: the 'instrument, pregnant ... with the fate of the world' has work yet to do. The powers of this man, ailing, months before his death, are still formidable and the incandescence of his desire to shape the course of human history continues to burn within his soul even if that revolutionary flame now appears to finally dim with age. But his pen, to the very end, never gave up its eloquence. As his apology continues, he writes:

> It adds sensibly to the sufferings of sickness to be deprived by it of a personal participation in the rejoicings of that day, ... I should, indeed, with peculiar delight, have met and exchanged there congratulations, personally, with the small band, the remnant of that host of worthies who joined with us on that day, in the bold and doubtful election we were to make, for our country, between submission and the sword; and to have enjoyed with them the consolatory fact that our fellow citizens, after half a century of experience and prosperity, continue to approve the choice we made.

The cadences of the scriptures are so deftly overlaid upon the rhetoric of democratic inclusiveness, perhaps beyond compare in the voluminous archive of public speaking in America, that a casual reading might overlook the millennial force of Jefferson's will to posterity. And while that will is, inevitably, focused upon his own standing in the history of the nation it nevertheless takes into its orbit the fate and continuing endurance of the republic itself. Not one to miss an opportunity for ennobling the actions of the revolutionary generation and his own participation in

the course of human events Jefferson brings the letter to a
rousing climax:

> May it be to the world, what I believe it will be, (to some
> parts sooner, to others later, but finally to all,) the signal
> of arousing men to burst the chains under which monkish
> ignorance and superstition had persuaded them to bind
> themselves, and to assume the blessings and security
> of self-government ... All eyes are opened or opening
> to the rights of man. The general spread of the light of
> science has already laid open to every view the palpable
> truth, that the mass of mankind has not been born with
> saddles on their backs, nor a favoured few, booted and
> spurred, ready to ride them legitimately by the grace of
> God. These are the grounds of hope for others; for our-
> selves, let the annual return of this day forever refresh
> our recollections of these rights, and an undiminished
> devotion to them.

By the time Jefferson wrote these magnificent sentences
they would have summoned up a set of associations – sounds,
smells, the unbidden guests allowed in by the visceral
somatic senses – that reeked of a distant far-off place, a time
that was *another century*. And while some people, though not
many, one suspects, might have picked up the fact that the
author had, once again, not striven for originality in expression – borrowing the words of one of Cromwell's soldiers,
Richard Rumbold, who had proclaimed from the scaffold: 'I
never could believe that Providence had sent a few men into
the world, ready booted and spurred to ride, and millions
ready saddled and bridled to be ridden' – this served only
to underscore the fact that an era had passed. For Jefferson

was, of course, a son of the Enlightenment, as deeply versed in its rhythms of conceptualisation and attuned to its pace as he was submerged in its learning. He was from that other century. But America in 1826 was another country.

All over the Union jubilee celebrations were planned with the same Janus-like motivations. The day was to be both commemorative, proudly exhibiting what it now had enshrined as the 'spirit of '76' and, at the same time, looking forwards, prospective, tentatively embracing what many thought or hoped would be a bright shining future for the first modern democratic republic.

The events that took place in Newark, New Jersey, that day are typical of Fourth celebrations all over the Union. Dawn brought the jangling resonances of clanging bells and the bursts of cannon fire. Sixty war veterans headed up the parade, many of them dressed in what they had preserved from their uniforms of the time. They carried muskets, powder horns or cartridge boxes from the same revolutionary campaign. Behind came the current young men who comprised the militia. And following their footsteps were the resident tailors, blacksmiths, carpenters, stone masons, cabinet makers, saddlers, shoe makers. Bringing up the rear the Committee of Arrangements proudly wore their caps of liberty and included within their ranks the orator and the person selected to read the Declaration. The procession made its way to a church which was to host the official speeches. On leaving the church the revolutionary veterans headed up a second procession which included teams of oxen dragging a fifty-foot obelisk that was to be erected as a monument to 'Independence and Government'. A second civic monument, called the 'Temple of Independence', was also dedicated that day on the town common. This structure comprised thirteen columns supporting a domed roof. The words 'Independence', 'Fourth of July', '1776', and 'Liberty and Equality' were inscribed around the top, and slightly lower around the outer ring of the dome ran a list of names of revolutionary war generals.

By 1826 Washington had become firmly established as the seat of the national government and it was fitting for the jubilee to be celebrated with considerable pomp in that city. No such plans were laid by the local representatives of the city which could stake a claim for being at the epicentre of the revolution, the city in which the nation's independence had been set in motion: Philadelphia. That year one of the most prominent Philadelphian newspapers reported that 'all was quiet' on the Fourth, and it went on to remark the 'apathy of the citizens'. Perhaps all eyes and ears were on the Capitol, where the second of the Adams family presidents was efficiently going about the business of government. On the morning of the celebrated day John Quincy Adams met at nine with his secretaries of War and of the Treasury without heed to the final preparations for the procession which were being made outside. The parade set off with cavalry, the militia, and a military band followed by the mayor and the orator for the day. The president joined the procession in a carriage which he shared with the members of the Committee of Arrangements. His vice-president, John C. Calhoun, from whom he was now politically estranged, rode behind in a second carriage. As had become customary the parade included the great and the good and, bringing up the rear the 'citizens and strangers' who were allowed in to the executive mansion following the official ceremonies. Perhaps the gesture that was to have most enduring significance, made by the sixth president on this day, was the planting of various trees – acorn, hickory and chestnut – in public spaces around the capital.

The real legacy of the jubilee, what it gave and continues to give to the story of the nation and what, even at the time, was understood as its enormous symbolic weight, is wound up in the interlocking lives and *punctual* deaths of two of the architects of the revolution, John Adams and Thomas Jefferson. Although both were facing their imminent decease each nevertheless strenuously gave his distinctive stamp to the story that was to emerge from the celebrations of the nation's jubilee. For what history has remembered is the romance, the breathtakingly apposite, punctual coincidence which saw these two grand men of '76 die on the very day of the nation's fiftieth birthday. And around that fact history has burnished and embellished what little we know about the final days and hours of these two presidents. It is this story, the interlinked narratives which comprise the lives and deaths of these two men, which enhances the symbolic power of the Fourth.

One should begin by recalling that these two men who had sat on the committee charged with the responsibility of drafting the Declaration, and seen it through the cut and thrust of congressional collective editing, had ended up on different sides of a political divide. Adams, the second president, had become a figurehead of sorts for the federalists while his successor to the presidency was one of the leading lights in the democratic-republican opposition. But in the last fourteen years of their lives they had repaired bridges and in the considerable volume of correspondence that flowed back and forth between them recovered a friendship that ran into the foundations of the nation's history. Although the public at large was, of course, not privy to that correspondence, both sides in the political landscape could, by 1826, respect each other's grand old man. It would be fair to say, then, that both were held in considerable affection by the time the jubilee was celebrated. All the more so given the ailing health of both men.

By 1818 the palsy from which Adams suffered had become sufficiently acute to prevent him from writing with any regularity. He had been blessed with good health for most of his life, give or take minor ailments, but now, entering his last eight years, the wear and tear of advancing age became far more evident. By the time the jubilee year kicked off he was almost blind, toothless and pretty much confined to the family home in Quincy. Notwithstanding the slow decrepitude he was experiencing, visitors during these last months spoke of his lively conversation and sharp mind, not to say occasionally sharp tongue for which he had become renowned as a young man promoting the cause of independence sixty years earlier. He had reason to be entering his final months and weeks in an equable state of mind: his first son was holding the pre-eminent office of the nation and he was surrounded by his extended, loyal and loving family.

Jefferson, now bankrupt, was still atop his hill at Monticello but also ailing. He too had been fortunate to live a life free from major illness but now the three or four hours a day in the saddle – a custom he had observed until his early seventies – were becoming very rare occurrences, all the more so since breaking his left arm at the age of sixty-eight. Now, entering his last year, he was suffering with chronic and debilitating digestive problems which prevented him from receiving visitors. But both men were determined to see their lives through to the day which loomed as the fitting terminus to their individual and collaborative odysseys.

'Argonauts', as Jefferson called the men of '76 in the last letter he wrote to Adams in March of the jubilee year, who had weathered the storm of 'our Argosy', the foundation of the first modern republic. Many alive in 1826 regarded the fact that both did, in fact, prevail until the day itself as the result of divine intervention. And from here on history takes over: all that follows from the remarkable coincidence that these two signatories to the declaration, the second and third presidents of the country, died within hours of each other on the day of the fiftieth anniversary of the nation's birth is now part of the story that is America.

Jefferson, according to one of the strands in this story, died at *the same hour* on the same day that the Declaration had first been read in Congress: 1.00 p.m. And on the day itself, 4 July 1826, only a few miles from his beloved Monticello, as he was taking his final gasps of air the Declaration was, once more, being read aloud in Charlottesville. Although the veracity of this story was far from universally credited – the *Albany Argus & Daily City Gazette*, for example, qualified the story, pointing out that the Declaration had been 'promulgated in the halls of Congress' at that hour, while it had first been read aloud at 'about a quarter before five o'clock' [10 July 1826] – it is the punctuality of the story of Jefferson's demise that so bewitched the nation. It was no secret that Jefferson had been very close to death for weeks – during the second half of June his doctor, a young Englishman named Robley Dunglison, had been summoned to help him through what appeared to be the final stretch of his life. By 2 July his digestive system was unable to deal with much in the way of sustenance. Laudanum helped alleviate the pain. But on the 3rd Jefferson roused from a delirium agitated about the Committee of Safety – 'Warn the Committee to be on the alert', he is supposed to have said. And all through that night, when he roused from fitful sleep, he inquired 'This is the Fourth?'

In a variant of this story Jefferson asks more than once if the day has arrived, enquiring of his interlocutor, Nicholas P. Trist, husband of his granddaughter Virginia Randolph Trist, 'Is it the Fourth?' Trist, not wanting to distress the dying man, is supposed to have replied in the affirmative even though he knew that the hour had not yet come. And then, with grace and resignation, the third president is claimed to have said 'Just as I wished'. So, to his dying words, whatever they were, this most self-fashioned man of the Enlightenment managed to arrange history the way he wanted. Thomas Jefferson, the author of the Declaration of Independence, willed his demise to coincide precisely within the very hour that marked the fiftieth anniversary of the nation he had been instrumental in bringing into existence.

Adams's legacy to history is no less characterised by the romance of the Fourth. By June that year he had become so weak that he rarely left the family home, even though his mental faculties remained in good order. On 3 July, for example, he is supposed to have been visited by Daniel Webster who inquired, 'How do you do this morning, Mr Adams?' to which the second president replied, 'Not very well. I am living in a very old house, Mr Webster, and, from all that I can learn, the landlord does not intend to repair.' As the day approached it became very clear that he would be lucky to survive and to be granted his wish of seeing it through to the day of the nation's jubilee. Although lucid right up through the first days of July his strength was diminishing almost hourly. On the night of the 3rd he appeared to be suffering and close to the end.

He awoke on the morning of the 4th to the sound of cannon firing off their salutes and a servant is supposed to have asked him if he knew what day it was. Adams, so history tells us, replied, 'O yes, it is the glorious fourth of July – God bless it – God bless you all'. Later in the morning the orator for the celebrations in Quincy, the Reverend John Whitney, paid this most illustrious citizen of the town a visit and asked the 91-one-year-old patriot if he had a 'sentiment' that might be conveyed to the massed audience who would be gathering for the oration. 'I will give it to you,' Adams said, 'Independence forever'. The old man's granddaughter, Susan B. Clark, asked if he had anything to add to this, 'Not a syllable', he replied.

According to another source, Judge William Cranch, a classmate of Adams's son John Quincy, the grand old man was fully cognisant of the day's unfolding. Cranch's story – he wrote a biography of Adams shortly after his death – was based on his acquaintance with those who were close to the family or indeed a part of it. In the account that Cranch published, at one point during the course of the day Adams proclaimed, 'It is a great and good day', indicating that 'his thoughts were dwelling on the scenes of 1776'. Then, as life ebbed away from one of the architects of the nation, Cranch gives us the punctual moment that has fallen into history. He claimed that 'the last words he uttered … were "Jefferson survives"'. It is not known who recorded these words – Cranch does not reveal his source – but the symbolic power of the story is such that it seems to compel belief anyway. Certainly Adams's son, John Quincy, wanted to believe it since he recorded in his diary entry for 21 July of that year that his father had spoken the words 'Thomas Jefferson survives' at 1.00 p.m. on the 4th.

Seen this way, an incredible accident of history occurred that day in 1826. At the precise moment when his old ally and venerable friend Thomas Jefferson, having for the last time refused the laudanum offered by his physician, was painfully taking his last gasps 450 or so miles away at his home in Monticello, John Adams uttered his very name. And *these* were the last words he, Adams, was himself to speak. It is unlikely that events transpired according to such perfect symmetry. It may well be that Adams's last words were these, but if so the coincidence of his speaking them at precisely the moment (or very close to it) that Jefferson died is hard to credit. We do not know if Adams sank into semi-consciousness following this last flickering of his powerful mind, but we do know that the time of his decease was around 5.30 p.m. It might be said that the precise detail really did not matter since the will to have it so, for the jubilee to be touched by a kind of divine providence, was in the ascendant. All over the country, as the news slowly spread, citizens were touched by the extraordinary finale to the lives of these remarkable men. And immediately on its tails the siren voice of history began to whisper in low seductive tones. Already by 16 July the story had become embellished with detail that people wanted to believe. In a sermon given that day in Washington by the former chaplain to the senate, William Staughton, we can find the building blocks of the legend already in place. 'Mr Jefferson', he claimed, 'expressed his wish to live until the day of Jubilee; his desire was granted him.' His friend 'Mr Adams, on hearing the voice of the cannon, and being informed that it announced the Jubilee of our Independence said, "O it is a great, a glorious day"; and spake no more.' Another account, this time put about by Samuel Smith in Baltimore, claimed that the last words of the venerable Adams were "Independence forever". The last words of our beloved Jefferson (let not his country forget them) were "I resign my Soul to my God, and My daughter to my country. And I humbly hope that this country will watch over and guard her, aid and cherish her".

And so, perhaps for all time, the strange conjunction in which two former presidents died within hours of each other on the day of the jubilee will cast its strange spell. Many Americans, from that day to this, have chosen to see in this unlikely fact the hand of something more than human. As Abraham Lincoln remarked in 1863 about the near simultaneous decease of the two great men: 'This extraordinary coincidence we can understand to be a dispensation of the Almighty Ruler of Events'. Whether one subscribes to this or not it remains the case that the legacy of the jubilee has been to reinforce the sense that the Fourth marks a singular moment in time, the *punctuality* of the birth of the nation.

3

THE SYMBOLS OF THE FOURTH

THE FLAG

History is full of accidents – small events prompted by the efforts of mainly insignificant actors which, by chance, may gain an importance undreamt of by their perpetrators. The spring day in March 1870 when a certain William Canby rose to his feet and addressed the Pennsylvania Historical Society is one such accident of history. 'Mr President, and gentlemen of the Historical Society of Pennsylvania,' he began. 'A number of persons, who, like yourselves are impressed with the importance of preserving every item of history relating to the origin of our beautiful national standard ...' And what then followed was to provide in both outline and detail the basis of a story that for generations has cast its compelling spell. A story which encapsulates the heroism of the founding of the nation. A story that *feels* right, even if the evidence for its detail is far from secure. In fact, according to the strictest protocols of historical inquiry, there is *no evidence* for the central claim made in Canby's lecture about the 'origin of our beautiful national standard'. It is a myth. It is, therefore, all the more intriguing that what has come down to us, the narrative that has been told and retold, has the air of a true story. It appears to make a claim on history. Why and how this came about is the subject of the first part of this chapter.

Canby was well aware of the difficulties he was about to encounter in his attempt to convince his audience that what he had to say was historically accurate. This is why he began his talk almost immediately with an account of the thorough archival research he had undertaken, demonstrating his *bona fides* as an amateur historian. Even so he was nevertheless forced to conclude with the admission that 'It is quite needless to detail the labors of this search, or to enumerate the works examined; suffice it to say that the result was as anticipated – the printed official record was found to stand, where it had been alleged to stand, bare and unsatisfying, involved in a mass of conjecture, with but one central point.' That one point lies within John Dunlap's *Journal of Congress*, dated 14 June 1777, where a record of the following resolution may be found: 'Resolved that the flag of the thirteen United States be thirteen stripes, alternate red and white; that the union be thirteen stars, white in a blue field, representing a new constellation.' This much is history. But it is the other material, the 'mass of conjecture', that has played the more significant role in the story of the nation's founding.

For in the remainder of his paper Canby spun a tale that has become familiar to millions of Americans over the intervening 140 years. A story that he claimed he had heard from its source, his grandmother, Betsy Ross. But, standing in front of his historian peers that day in March 1870, he knew that questions would be raised about the accuracy of his own memory. It was bound to be pointed out, for example, that he had been only eleven years of age at the time of his conversation with his grandmother. So, being an enthusiastic amateur historian, he had set about gathering sworn affidavits from those surviving family members who had recollections of Betsy's story. All of them told, roughly, the same story. The story Canby had now come to deliver as fact, that his grandmother, Betsy Ross, had been approached by a secret committee comprising George Washington, Robert Morris and George Ross and asked to 'make the first star spangled banner that was ever made', as his aunt, Margaret Boggs, put it in her sworn affidavit.

Canby knew that parts of this story were going to be hard to sell. In the first place, as he had admitted in his preamble to the paper he presented, there is no record of a secret committee of three charged with responsibility for commissioning a flag in any documents relating to the Second Continental Congress. This in itself is not particularly noteworthy since, as we have seen, written records for those proceedings are very rudimentary. For good reason, of course, since the colonists were meeting to discuss matters that could lead to the charge of treason. There is also the minor problem of chronology. According to Canby's relatives Washington et al. called on Betsy some time before the Second Continental Congress had issued its Declaration of Independence. Why, then, would it have need of a flag? This is further complicated by the fact that we *do* have documentary evidence for the resolution made by Congress on 14 June 1777 in which a new flag for the then fledgling nation was proposed. And, to make matters worse, there is no record whatsoever of Washington having been appointed to *any* committee of the Congress, secret or otherwise – which can be explained by the simple fact that he was not a member of that body; he was, rather, beholden to it.

Canby, however, was not to be thrown off his track. He had, after all, heard the story told in its variants by many family members, and there was one version, sworn to under oath in June 1870 as testimony by another aunt, Rachel

Fletcher, which seemed to convey an undeniable truth. It was so full of colour, detail, lived experience. And, given that it was Betsy's own daughter speaking, how could one raise a sceptical eyebrow to such an authoritative source? Fletcher, referring to her mother by her last married name, Claypoole, swore that 'I remember having heard my mother Elizabeth Claypoole say frequently that she, with her own hands, (while she was the widow of John Ross,) made the first Star-spangled Banner that ever was made. I remember to have heard her also say that it was made on the order of a Committee, of whom Col. Ross was one, and that Robert Morris was also one of the Committee.'

Fletcher's testimony essentially covers the same ground as that sworn to by Margaret Boggs, but it is fuller, pungently smelling of historical veracity. And much of the detail in it provides seed for the later flowering of the full-blown Betsy Ross story. Fletcher, for example, introduces the fact that Betsy was connected to the congressional committee by marriage – her husband was the nephew of Colonel George Ross. This seemingly innocuous detail will later prove to be one of the supports for the credibility of the story since it helps explain how it came to pass that Betsy, rather than anyone else in Philadelphia, had been given the historic commission to make the first flag.

Fletcher herself seemed to be sensitive to the objection that the connection between her mother and some of the prominent leaders of the revolution – indeed with the first president – was far fetched. In order to head off such qualms she stated that Betsy 'was previously well acquainted with Washington, and that he had often been in her house in friendly visits, as well as on business'. It turned out that her mother 'had embroidered ruffles for his shirt bosoms and cuffs, and that it was partly owing to his friendship for her that she was chosen to make the flag'. How this came about is revealed in the following account of Washington's visit to Betsy's modest parlour, a story which has captured the imagination of generations of Americans and is familiar from countless grade-school lessons. According to Fletcher, Washington and his colleagues 'showed [Betsy] a drawing roughly executed, of the flag as it was proposed to be made by the committee', but her mother 'saw in it some defects in its proportions and the arrangement and shape of the stars'. Betsy opined that 'it was square and a flag should be one third longer than its width'; furthermore, 'the stars were scattered promiscuously over the field, and she said they should be either in lines or in some adopted form as a circle, or a star, and ... the stars were six-pointed in the drawing, and she said they should be five pointed'. Washington and his colleagues were grateful for the suggestions 'and acted upon them, General Washington seating himself at a table with a pencil and paper, altered the drawing and then made a new one according to the suggestions of my mother'. Fletcher adds that 'General Washington seemed to her to be the active one in making the design, the others having little or nothing to do with it'.

As this story has been handed down it has attracted incidental elements or slightly different emphases – in one version, for example, Betsy had already had some experience in flag making, although according to her daughter this was, in fact, a new departure. This is why Washington and his two colleagues suggested that Betsy call on another member of the Congress, a shipping merchant in the city, who, they said, would be able to supply her with a flag that she could imitate. Betsy duly visited the merchant – Fletcher adds the colourful detail that her mother had been 'punctual to her appointment' – and he 'drew out of a chest an old ship's color which he loaned her to show her how the sewing was done'.

In the meantime Washington's design, now approved by Betsy and Congress, had been supplied to a local artist so that a watercolour could be painted and then worked from in the manufacture of the flag. Fletcher adds another significant detail to this part of the story, noting that William Barrett, the commissioned artist, 'lived on the North side of Cherry Street above Third Street, a large three story brick house on the West side of an alley which ran back to the Pennsylvania Academy for Young Ladies kept by James A. Neal, the best school of the kind in the city at that time'.

Perhaps at this point in his lecture Canby noticed his audience becoming restive. He was almost certainly aware of a problem looming on the horizon, since even if his aunt's testimony was accurate how could one be sure that the design for the eventual flag was in fact his grandmother's and not the artist William Barrett's? So it was with some relief that he was able to provide from his aunt's affidavit evidence that this potentially damaging alternative hypothesis about the source of the nation's most potent symbol was insecure. For Rachel Fletcher swore that 'Barrett only did the painting, and had nothing to do with the design' – adding for good measure that 'he was often employed by mother afterwards to paint the coats of arms of the United States and of the States on silk flags'.

Why is Betsy's story, in all its incidental colour, so tightly woven into the fabric of the larger narrative that is the history of the nation's founding? What is the character of its form or structure which enables it to be tied so comfortably to the other narrative strands which collectively tell the story of the birth of the nation? Does each of these discrete elements – the signing of the Declaration, the manufacture of the first flag, the story of the Liberty Bell – have a common narrative imprint which helps build the larger story that is 'America's birthday'? Although it would be wrong to suggest that the Betsy Ross legend provides *the* template for all the different stories about the founding of the nation – some of them predate the account of the flag rehearsed above by nearly a century – it does, nevertheless, enable us to see quite clearly how they all share a common narrative shape. How they all bear the imprint of a single storyline about origination and innovation, about the creation of something from scratch. Let's call it the ideology of 'America'.

Motivating the narrative grammar of Betsy's story is a desire to describe or establish a unique founding moment, a singular event which brings together various strands of her story – key players in the history of the new republic, local (and unknown) tradespeople, the skills of a single seamstress – into a punctual moment: the creation of the symbol that will speak for the nation, its flag. Like many of the individual narratives which comprise the larger story of the nation it has an heroic individual – Betsy – at its heart. Much of the incidental detail in the Betsy Ross legend is there in order to help us form a picture of this heroine, to both humanise her and venerate her achievement. And it is, of course, of signal importance that our heroine is merely a representative of the common weal, not a member of the ruling elite or the professional class. She is testament to the fact that each citizen has equal opportunity, equal rights, equal potential to become a significant player in the history of the nation. This is what William Canby wanted to believe and why his story about his grandmother feels credible: it is one example of what the narrative code driving all stories of American exceptionalism can produce. It was the same code, deeply embedded in the third president's capacious learning and intelligence, which gave a shape and form to the story he fashioned of his own life and the part it played in the nation's founding. And like any generative grammar it has the capacity to produce both stories which help bring about the fruition of universal aspirations as well as those which prevent them from being realised.

To this day there are those who insist that the Betsy Ross story is not a myth, that although the historical record cannot provide enough material to corroborate it according to the standards of professional historians there is nevertheless the 'grain of truth' within it. And in a curious way they are right. For it hardly matters if it is true or not, since common sense dictates that *someone* must have run up the first standard that was adopted by the new nation, and some person, or group of persons, must have designed the flag that was subsequently manufactured. What harm can there be in accepting *this* story as the moment of origin for the national standard if no other makes a similar claim?

In fact there is a rival account. One of the signers of the Declaration, Francis Hopkinson, who designed the seal for the Board of Admiralty, claimed in a letter of 25 May 1780 that he also supplied designs for 'The Flag of the United States of America'. Hopkinson had provided these gratis – referring to them as 'labours of fancy' – but now, in 1780, he was inquiring whether or not Congress might see fit to express its gratitude in the form of some pecuniary gesture. But this story hardly even gets to flicker across the screen of history. Almost from the day Canby stood up to address his audience in Philadelphia Betsy's story is the one that has been accepted as fact, or if not exactly fact at least a fable that is as good as fact.

In the July 1873 issue of *Harper's Monthly* the story was told again and soon afterwards it began to appear in text-books used in schools all over the country. Today one can visit Betsy's house in Philadelphia and see the rooms in which she supposedly cut her five-pointed star. Or, if only a virtual visit is possible, there is a website devoted to maintaining the fable – indeed, it is devoted to dispelling the cruel slander that it *is* a fable. Others have also corroborated parts of the story. Samuel Wetherill, a good friend of Betsy and along with her one of the last two members of the Free Quaker Meeting House which closed in 1834, had his own story to tell. This, a tale also passed down like an heirloom through the generations, has it that the original five-pointed star which Betsy had cut out of paper in front of George Washington survives. According to Wetherill family lore, Samuel visited Betsy shortly after she had been commissioned by the secret congressional committee to make the flag. She told him what had just transpired. Wetherill, recognising the historic import of that meeting, asked if he could keep the five-pointed star which she had cut and she complied with his request. Then, just short of 150 years later in 1925, the family safe belonging to the Wetherill family was opened and inside was found a five-pointed star. One can still see it today exhibited at the Free Quaker Meeting House, a few blocks away from the Betsy Ross House.

The veneration of such objects and the stories woven around them has parallels with the narratives we find in another important area of human experience: religious observance. Trees that shed blood, shrouds bearing the image of Christ, relics of dozens of saints and holy people have all, at various times, become talismanic objects for observers of various religious faiths. And why should it not be so for the continuing belief in the ideals of the revolutionary generation? In one sense the Betsy Ross story is part of a larger fabric which renews and sustains Americans' commitment to the lofty humanistic principles which were embedded in the Declaration of Independence. The Founding Fathers, Jefferson the principal among them, were deeply suspicious of any state interference in religious observance and sought to maintain a clear separation between government and church. But they were not averse to the ideals of their revolution being revered *as if* they constituted articles of faith. Indeed, in the long struggle to create and prolong into futurity a new kind of nation, a state founded on the principle of inalienable human rights, something like a religious fervour was and is required. And it is this, above all else, that survives to this day: the commitment to an ideal that is as deeply humanistic as any that has ever been articulated. It is hardly surprising, then, that in the spirit of the Enlightenment that moved the Founding Fathers, stories have been used to memorialise the heroic actions of those who played a part in the founding of the nation. And each year, on 4 July, all citizens are given the opportunity to express their consent to the grand project initiated in Philadelphia in 1776.

It is also hardly surprising, given the role that the flag plays in the founding myths of the nation, that over time this object more than any other has aroused passions. At the time of the revolution flags were, of course, a common feature of social and political life. They were especially evident on the battlefield or at sea, as they had been for centuries. But in the development of the modern state they have taken on wider significance. And during the bitter struggle of the Civil War the flag became the primary means of identification for one's political allegiance. But it was not until the early twentieth century that measures were adopted by Congress to give special prominence to the national flag.

'Flag Day' had been observed on 14 June by communities across the United States for decades prior to 1916, but on 30 May that year President Wilson proposed that it become a punctual moment in the calendar of the nation. 'It has seemed to me fitting', he said,

> that I should call your attention to the approach of the anniversary of the day upon which the Flag of the United States was adopted by the Congress as the emblem of the Union, and to suggest to you that it should this year and the years to come be given special significance ...
>
> I therefore suggest and request that throughout the nation, and, if possible, in every community, the four-teenth day of June be observed as FLAG DAY, with special patriotic exercises, at which means shall be taken to give significant expression to our thoughtful love of America ... our determination to make it greater and purer ...

Seven years later the first National Flag Conference was held in Washington, DC on, appropriately enough, 14 June, Flag Day. Part of the business of the conference was to adopt a National Flag Code, a set of prescriptions pertaining to the use of the national emblem. Representatives of both the navy and the army attended, as did delegates from some sixty-six other national groups. The aim was to agree upon a common code of conduct for the flag. A year later a few minor changes were made to this code at the second National

Flag Conference. Eighteen years after that, on 22 June 1942, Congress passed a joint resolution, subsequently amended on 22 December 1942, which now comprises Public Law 829; Chapter 806, 77th Congress, 2nd session. Exact rules for use and display of the flag (36 U.S.C. 173–178) as well as associated sections (36 U.S.C. 171) covering the Conduct during Playing of the National Anthem, (36 U.S.C. 172), the Pledge of Allegiance to the Flag, and its Manner of Delivery. The preamble to this document reads:

> This code is the guide for all handling and display of the Stars and Stripes. **It does not impose penalties** for misuse of the United States Flag. That is left to the states and to the federal government for the District of Columbia. Each state has its own flag law.

Of course, one of the cherished political instruments of the United States is the separation of federal from state legislatures; for many it is precisely this separation which keeps the Union together, precisely this devolution of legislative power which keeps the Union strong. So it should be no surprise that each state has evolved its own flag law. There are, nevertheless, statutory penalties for certain acts of desecration to the flag which are upheld by federal law and are contained in Title 18 of the United States Code. In 1989 a challenge was made to this statute and ruled upon by the Supreme Court in its decision *Texas* v. *Johnson*, by which it held the statute unconstitutional. This led the legislature to amend the statute in its Flag Protection Act of 1989 (Oct. 28, 1989). According to this redrawn legislation a fine and/or up to one year in prison could be imposed for 'knowingly mutilating, defacing, physically defiling, maintaining on the floor or trampling upon any flag of the United States'. Less than a year later the Flag Protection Act of 1989 was struck down by the Supreme Court decision, *United States* v. *Eichman*, decided on 11 June 1990. It was stated in this ruling that, 'While the Code empowers the President of the United States to alter, modify, repeal or prescribe additional rules regarding the Flag, no federal agency has the authority to issue "official" rulings legally binding on civilians or civilian groups.' It is for this reason that 'different interpretations of various provisions of the Code may continue to be made' and that 'The Flag Code may be fairly tested'. In conclusion it noted that 'actions not specifically included in the Code may be deemed acceptable as long as proper respect is shown'.

In spite of this ruling, since 1995 the House of Representatives has periodically – in fact every two years – proposed an amendment to the Constitution 'authorizing the Congress to prohibit the physical desecration of the flag of the United States'. Each time – at least up until the time of this writing – the proposal has come before the Senate it has been defeated. Why should this issue continue to raise such heated debate in a mature democracy? Why, indeed, is it felt necessary to protect a piece of cloth? The answer to these questions can be found in the common narrative architecture which supports the various stories told about the founding of America. For that architecture seeks to encourage if not produce a particular form of address – call it an attitude or stance – to objects, ideals or even stories which, on account of their quasi-sacred status, require one to demonstrate good manners in their company. Ideals such as 'truths held to be sacred and undeniable', as Jefferson had first written in his draft of the Declaration. And the flag has become one of these strange secular objects. In the words of the cultural historian Wilbur Zelinsky it has 'pre-empted the place, visually and otherwise, of the crucifix in older Christian lands'. Such a view was explicitly encouraged by a number of protest groups around the turn of the nineteenth century who took it upon themselves to mount a campaign to protect the flag. According to Charles Kingsbury Miller, one of the most prominent campaigners and author of a book entitled *The Crime of the Century: Desecration of the American Flag* published in 1900, the nation needed to look out for 'those three sacred jewels, the Bible, the Cross and the Flag'. The last most especially since unscrupulous businessmen had 'polluted' the flag 'whose sacred folds were never designed to be defaced with advertisements of beer, sauerkraut, candy, itch ointment, pile remedies and patent nostrums'. One of his colleagues even went so far as to claim that the flag could be compared to the 'Holy of Holies'. Lest this be thought of as a peculiar idiosyncrasy of early twentieth-century Americans a more recent expression of the same view was uttered by the Louisiana Democratic representative Hale Boggs in 1967 when he described flag desecration as 'outrageous acts which go beyond protest and violate things which the overwhelming majority of Americans hold sacred'. No wonder, then, that acts of disrespect to the flag cause deep distress to so many people.

For the same reason the United States has developed a far more elaborate set of 'Guidelines for Displaying the Flag' than any other modern nation. These guidelines run as follows:

1. The flag of the United States should be flown daily from sunrise to sunset in good weather from public buildings, schools, permanent staffs, and in or near

polling places on election days. The flag may be displayed 24 hours a day on patriotic holidays or if properly illuminated.

2. The flag should not be displayed on days when the weather is bad, except when an all-weather flag is used.

3. The flag should always be flown on national and state holidays and on those occasions proclaimed by the President. On Memorial Day, the flag should be half staffed until noon.

4. The flag should be hoisted briskly and lowered ceremoniously. It should never be dipped to any person nor should it ever be displayed with the union down, except as a signal of great distress.

5. The flag should never touch anything beneath it, nor should it ever be carried flat or horizontally.

6. It should never be used as wearing apparel, bedding, drapery, or decoration, nor for carrying or holding anything.

7. The flag should never be fastened, displayed, used, or stored in such a manner as to be easily torn, soiled, or damaged. It should never be used as a covering for a ceiling.

8. The flag should not be draped over the hood, top, sides, or back of a vehicle. When a flag is displayed on a car, the flag's staff should be fixed firmly to the chassis or clamped to the right fender.

9. The flag or its staff should never be used for advertising purposes in any manner whatsoever. Nor should any picture, drawing, insignia or other decoration be placed on or attached to the flag, its staff or halyard.

10. The flag should not be embroidered on cushions,

handkerchiefs, or other personal items nor printed on anything designed for temporary use and discarded. However, a flag patch may be affixed to the uniform of military personnel, firemen, policemen, or members of other patriotic organizations.

11. When the flag is so worn or soiled that it is no longer suitable for display, it should be destroyed in a dignified manner, preferably by burning.

It makes sense to see these provisions in a slightly longer historical perspective since from the late nineteenth century Americans have been pledging allegiance to the flag in a ritual that performs one's citizenship. The words which comprise the pledge were originally published in 1892, in the 8 September issue of *The Youth's Companion*, the then leading family magazine. Its author was Francis Bellamy, a Baptist minister. Bellamy had been a chairman of a committee of state superintendents of education in the National Education Association and had been in charge of designing the programme for the public schools' quadricentennial celebration of Columbus Day in 1892. He created a flag-raising ceremony for this occasion and wrote the pledge as a salute to be given the flag as it was raised. His original read:

I pledge allegiance to my Flag and the Republic for which it stands, one Nation, indivisible, with Liberty and Justice for all.

His initial impulse had been to use word 'equality' as well as liberty and justice but he was keenly aware that many of the state superintendents of education were opposed to equality for women and African-Americans. In October 1892 the word 'to' was inserted between 'and the' so that it read: 'and to the republic for which it stands'.

In 1923, on the occasion of the first National Flag Conference held in Washington, DC, the wording was again altered so that it read: 'I pledge allegiance to the Flag of the United States'. This alteration was against the wishes of Bellamy. The following year a further alteration was made so that it then read: 'I pledge allegiance to the flag of the United States of America'. In this form the pledge became an unofficial daily ritual in schools across America for nearly twenty years before Congress included it in the United States Flag Code (Title 36) on 22 June 1942. The year following the Supreme Court ruled that schoolchildren could not be forced to recite the pledge as part of their daily routine. Two years after this, in 1945, it was officially designated as 'The Pledge of Allegiance'.

In 1954 a campaign initiated by the Roman Catholic Knights of Columbus brought a bill to amend the pledge to Congress. Senator Homer Ferguson of Michigan sponsored the bill, claiming that the proposed addition of the words 'under God' would officially distinguish the United States from the atheist Soviet Union, and at the same time would remove any ambiguity that the pledge was instrumental in encouraging flag or nation worship. Congress assented to this proposal and on 14 June 1954 President Dwight D. Eisenhower passed into law the formula which now reads: 'I pledge allegiance to the Flag of the United States of America, and to the Republic for which it stands: one Nation under God, indivisible, with Liberty and Justice for all.'

Since then it has not all been plain sailing: in 2002 the California ninth circuit appellate court upheld a ruling that the words 'under God' were unconstitutional. This particular interpretation of constitutional rights provoked a reaction in Congress which sought to reverse the decision by unanimously calling for a further test of the case. Senator Bob Smith of New Hampshire had, after all, only as recently as 1999 sponsored a resolution which was duly passed in the Senate that the Pledge be recited before each day's session of the House. Consequently, following the 2002 ruling in the appellate court the case was indeed brought before the Supreme Court. It is important to note that the original case had come to the California court in a slightly unusual manner: it was claimed that the rights of the young girl who had been required to recite the pledge had been infringed. The case was founded on the observation that it was unconstitutional to induct this girl into any form of religious observance and not that the words 'under God' were in themselves a breach of constitutional rights. The claim, however, was not made by the girl but by her father, who brought it on her behalf. The subsequent Supreme Court decision ducked its responsibilities in respect of the soundness of the law regarding the pledge by – rather disingenuously – throwing the case out on a technical ground. During the proceedings it was revealed that the individual who had brought the case on behalf of his daughter was in fact not the legal guardian of the girl – her parents had divorced and she now lived with her mother and stepfather. Given this, the court ruled that her biological father could not, therefore, bring the case on her behalf. This leaves in suspension, as of 2007, whether or not there may be subsequent actions brought against the inclusion of the words which were said to be contra constitutional rights.

It is, perhaps, unsurprising that others, holding more mainstream political views, have proposed their own amendments to the pledge so that it might become more in keeping with their beliefs. One such unofficial pledge has it thus: 'I pledge allegiance to the Flag of the United States, and to the Republic for which it stands, one nation under God, indivisible, with liberty and justice for all, born and unborn', while another seeks to return to Bellamy's original intentions by reciting: 'I pledge allegiance to the Flag of the United States, and to the Republic for which it stands, one nation, indivisible, with equality, liberty and justice for all.' And of course the internet is clogged up with all manner of alternative suggestions which chime with whatever current injustice or curtailment of freedom seems to animate particular interest groups. But in what may often feel to some extent like opportunistic petitioning there remains a conceptual knot, a curious feature of the pledge and its symbolic ritual, that is brought out when one attends very closely to the words. For what is stated is that the flag *stands for* the republic.

What does this mean? How should we understand that a flag *stands for* a political entity? It is clearly not a *representation* of that entity, but nor is it, strictly speaking, a *symbol* of the first modern republic. Flags are counters in the languages which animate collective activities of many kinds: they have semiotic functions, encoded in the visual presentation of their design, which are precisely legible within the communicative contexts in which they are used – ship to ship, for example. Regiments march to flags, friendly societies advertise their existence by hoisting flags, nations adopt flags and impartial observers in war seek the protection of flags. But in all these cases the *material* out of which the flag is made does not have a peculiar *immaterial* status. Again, in all these cases the flag is symbolic, it stands for something else. But in the ritual of the pledge and enshrined in the Flag Code there is something else at work, a kind of sacralisation process which raises the flag from mere symbol to something *beyond the symbolic*. For the flag does not merely *stand for* the republic. In some strange way it *is* the republic. It is the nation. Both a unique object – *the* official flag whose form is designated in law, whose manufacture requires the use of a unique dye (called OG red, where 'OG' stands for 'Old Glory') – and at the same time a common property. As the Dallas County Assistant DA, Kathi Drew, claimed in the case Texas brought against Gregory Lee Johnson for the desecration of a 'venerated object' (the flag) and which was to lead to the Supreme Court's overruling of the conviction, the flag 'was public property in which every American had a stake'. She went on to claim that it 'is simply different from anything else, it is unique' and 'really belongs to the nation as a whole'. In her view this is why a constitutional amendment is required in order to protect such a 'unique entity'. It is also why there has been such careful attention paid to the correct way physically to address the flag while making the pledge.

Before the Second World War the pledge was initiated with the right hand over the heart while the phrase 'I pledge allegiance' was uttered. The arm was then extended towards the flag at the moment when the phrase 'to the flag' was uttered, and then it remained outstretched throughout the rest of the recitation, with the palm facing upward, as if to lift the flag. An earlier version of this salute, called the Bellamy salute, began with the right hand in a military salute, not over the heart. But during the war the outstretched arm became associated with the Nazi and fascist salutes so the physical orientation was altered. Thereafter, and continuing to this day, the pledge has been made with the hand over the heart from beginning to end. There are, however, other provisions. US

Customs, 36, Section 172 states that persons are expected, though not legally required, to recite the pledge 'By standing at attention facing the flag with the right hand over the heart'. It adds that 'When not in uniform men should remove their headdress with their right hand and hold it at the left shoulder, the hand being over the heart.' Those in uniform 'should remain silent, face the flag, and render the military salute.'

No matter how one understands these various protocols and provisions it remains the case that the words of the pledge give a particular prominence to the flag itself. They begin: 'I pledge allegiance to the flag of the United States', not 'I pledge allegiance to the republic and its flag' or some such other formulation. First to the flag *and then* to the republic for which it stands. First to the thing itself, and then to its symbolic designator. Perhaps this is why, over the last two centuries or so, US citizens have, from time to time, become concerned with the sanctity of the material of the flag itself.

There are many Stars and Stripes. Not only has the design of the flag been altered frequently – as every schoolchild knows, the number of stars has been increased each time another state has been admitted to the Union – there are also a significant number of flags which have had starring roles in moments of the nation's history: the flag, for example, that was used to rest Lincoln's head following the shot which killed him. The man who grabbed this makeshift cushion, Thomas Gourlay, kept the flag throughout his life and bequeathed it to his daughter, who in turn passed it on to her son, V. Paul Stuthers of Pike County, Pennsylvania. And he donated this sacred object to the Pike County Historical Society whose museum, The Columns, displays it to the present day. A flag with a more sentimental aura is that believed to be the first 'Old Glory' which sits protected under glass in the Smithsonian in Washington, DC. This flag originally belonged to William Driver, a sea captain, who had been given it by his mother and a group of girls from his home town of Salem. Driver is said to have exclaimed on opening his present, 'I name her Old Glory', and thereby another singular material example of the common property of the nation was born.

But perhaps the single most venerated piece of cloth in the nation's repository of sacred objects is the flag deemed to be *the* Star-spangled Banner. This flag has a long and curious pedigree that is entwined in the story of how the words that were to become the national anthem came to be written. The author of this text, Francis Scott Key, had been kept prisoner on board a vessel outside Baltimore during the war with Britain in 1814. He had observed from afar the British attempt to take Fort McHenry, which had flown an enormous flag, 32 feet by 43, throughout the battle. Key anxiously looked on, every so often remarking that the Stars and Stripes continued to fly above the fort, and his experience provided the material for a poem whose words were later put to a tune. That flag, made by Mary Pickersgill and her daughter Caroline, has since been designated as the first example of an American flag which can claim to be a Star-spangled Banner. It is held in such veneration, indeed it is the most popular exhibit in the Smithsonian Museum, that it is currently undergoing a restoration programme costing millions of dollars.

Just as the Fourth celebrates the birth of the nation, so Flag Day celebrates the birth of the flag. As we have seen, we do not know when *the flag* that has evolved into the pre-eminent symbol for the nation was first made, or by whom.

But there is a story, a good one with elements of other stories of founding, that conveys why this strange combination of a material thing, the weave of stained and sewn cloth, and an idea, an expression of the American mind, ought to be venerated. As President Woodrow Wilson eloquently conveyed to the nation on Flag Day in 1917, the symbolic power of the flag lies in its openness, its capaciousness. Just as the rituals of the Fourth are open to each generation's inflections of their meanings, so the flag and the republic for which it stands is a work in progress. This, at least, was Wilson's message, which began: 'We meet to celebrate Flag Day because this flag which we honor and under which we serve is the emblem of our unity, our power, our thought and purpose as a nation.' And he went on to make the explicit point that 'it has no other character than that which we give it from generation to generation. The choices are ours. It floats in majestic silence above the hosts that execute those choices, whether in peace or in war.'

Then, conveying something of the affection, even the affective power of an attachment to this common expression of identity, he said: 'And yet, though silent, it speaks to us – speaks to us of the past, of the men and women who went before us and of the records they wrote upon it. We celebrate the day of its birth ...' These sentiments are deeply held and they lie deep within the senses of being American. They are part of the foundations for the architecture of belief given expression in the declaration made each Fourth of July. This is why the story of the flag is caught up in a larger narrative of origination, why, for example, it becomes significant that the first flag ever explicitly designed for a nation (as distinguished from a monarch or other ruler) was the Stars and Stripes. America, seen from within the matrix of these founding stories, is the first modern nation. And that is worth celebration.

One very prominent effect of the story of the flag is the strange *extra symbolic* power it seems to grant to the material itself, creating an ability to bring comfort in times of great distress. Although there are many reasons behind the unprecedented surge in sales of Stars and Stripes following the attacks of 11 September 2001 – in a single day following the event Wal-Mart sold 118,000 flags – one of them is the lived and living experience of the motto stamped on the nation's seal: *e pluribus unum*. Carolyn Albanese, head of customer services at one of the largest manufacturers of American flags, Annin & Co., reported that following the attacks, 'People were calling us almost in a panic. They didn't just want to buy flags, they *needed* flags.' As if to help assuage such a national craving the US Postal Service provided one billion stamps with the flag on them to its post offices by 1 November 2001.

The story of the flag, of its origin, how it was made and who ran up the first example helps us to understand how it came about that a piece of cloth may be *beyond* meaning. In a secular world it provides evidence for – and often is the occasion for – a kind of veneration that comes into existence with the founding of a republic. When one takes up this attitude of respect or veneration, demanded by something that has gone beyond the sacred, one in effect performs something – call it a pledge or a declaratory act – which indicates a subscription to the notion that some truths are self-evident. And that is why the myth of Betsy Ross's first flag continues to be told and retold.

THE LIBERTY BELL

While there are countless material examples of the Stars and Stripes, millions of American flags, there is only one Liberty Bell. In this case the material that is the bell – the cast iron and copper which comprises its material form – has, through the strange process of symbolisation, taken on quasi-mystical properties. Over the centuries it has become venerated as a sacred object – in fact it already had acquired the symbolic value of the Ark of the Covenant by 1777 when the British occupied Philadelphia. In September of that year the bell was taken down from its tower and removed in a train comprising several hundred wagons and over 200 Virginian and North Carolinian soldiers to Allentown, Pennsylvania, for safe keeping. How did a very heavy lump of cast metal become the object of such veneration?

The bell was originally cast by one of the period's celebrated foundrymen, Thomas Lester of Whitechapel, whose foundry would also cast the bell that sits atop the bell tower in the Palace of Westminster, known affectionately as Big Ben. The foundry in east London is still in operation today. Lester was instructed by Robert Charles, the colonial agent for the province of Pennsylvania in London. And Charles had received his instruction from the three superintendents – Isaac Norris, Thomas Leech and Edward Warner – of the Philadelphia State House who had written to him in late 1751. A year or so earlier, in January 1750, two years after the completion of the State House, the assembly decided that the building needed a tower with a bell that might be rung on significant occasions as well as on those days when town meetings took place. Work on the tower was almost complete when, on 15 October 1751, another assembly meeting discussed the final touches for the tower and the possibility of commissioning the casting of a bell. The speaker of the assembly was Isaac Norris and he, along with the other two superintendents, was given the task of ordering 'a bell of such weight and dimensions as they shall think suitable'. Since, at that time, no large bell had been cast anywhere in the colonies the three superintendents were obliged to arrange for a bell to be made back in the mother country. A letter was duly dispatched to the province's agent, requesting that he procure 'a good bell of about 2,000 pounds weight'.

During 1751 the residents of Philadelphia were celebrating the fiftieth anniversary of William Penn's Charter of Privileges to the Province of Pennsylvania, so when it came to designing the bell it is possible that Norris, who was a scholarly man with sound knowledge of both Hebrew and Latin, was drawn to the verse in the Bible in which the people of Israel are encouraged to hold a jubilee every fifty years to celebrate their liberation from Egypt. The text of Leviticus reads: 'And ye shall hallow the fiftieth year, and proclaim liberty throughout all the land unto all the inhabitants thereof'. Whether or not the local celebrations were the prompt it is the case that the last clause of this sentence was chosen as a fitting inscription for the bell. In the letter of instruction sent to Robert Charles the superintendents requested that the following words 'well shaped in large letters' be inscribed around the crown of the bell: PROCLAIM LIBERTY THROUGHOUT THE LAND UNTO ALL THE INHABITANTS THEREOF. LEV. XXV.

The power of words to move people, to raise aspirations or commemorate great acts, does not lie only in the words themselves. Context is, of course, a significant contributor to the force and energy conveyed by any saying, and such contexts need not be originative. As is indeed the case with the Liberty Bell. The good people of Philadelphia could not have known in 1751 that twenty-five years later the thirteen colonies would rise up and with a clear voice declare themselves free citizens. Nor that the city of Philadelphia would host the Congress at which the Declaration of Independence would be agreed. But history is perforated with contingency. The power and force of the Liberty Bell, its *symbolic* power is not, however, an accident of history. It is the result of a set of narrative strategies which have invested the material object with a form of ahistorical force, a meaning that is not bound to a singular historical event or period. A set of narratives which removed it from its historical location, thereby transforming the object into a symbol encapsulating the ideals of the revolution.

We can follow those narrative strategies quite closely. It all began with the story of a flaxen-haired youth whose role in the proceedings on 4 July 1776 could not, at the time, have been predicted as particularly significant. This unknown boy, so the story goes, was charged with the responsibility of conveying the message that independence had been declared by the delegates to the Second Continental Congress to the people at large. And he was to do this by running from the chamber and shouting up to an old man who stood next to the bell in the bell tower: 'Ring! Ring!' And with that the Liberty Bell became a kind of narrative envelope into which the real thing, the bell itself, would be retroactively inserted. And once there, within the curtilage of its narrative form, it would be cut free from its own historical location and turned into something far more enduring: a symbolic marker conveying for all time the aspiration for freedom. This fictional enclave or narrative envelope, in slightly fuller detail, first came to public notice in the Philadelphia *Saturday Courier* of

1847 which published a short story entitled 'Fourth of July, 1776' by George Lippard, at the time a popular Philadelphia writer. And it was subsequently collected in his *Legends of the Revolution*. Not long after, the historian Beson J. Lossing began compiling his authoritative *The Pictorial Field Book of the Revolution*, in which he gathered together salient facts about the revolutionary period. And, ever since, the story made up by Lippard has assumed an air of authenticity, told and retold in school primers, handed down as lore from generation to generation.

In its more embellished form it goes like this. The moment the Second Continental Congress had resolved to declare independence from the mother country John Hancock, the president of that Congress, ordered that the bell in the tower of what is now called Independence Hall be rung and the articles of the Declaration be read aloud. His message was delivered by an unnamed flaxen-haired boy to an old man who stood at the top of the tower, next to the bell, awaiting his instruction: 'Ring!' It was this same boy who had, earlier in the afternoon, mounted the stairs to the bell tower and read aloud the inscription on the bell to the old man, who had found it difficult to discern the words. The young boy had obliged the elder townsman by reading: 'Proclaim liberty throughout all the land and unto all the inhabitants thereof'. And from here began the transformation of the bell struck in Whitechapel into the Liberty Bell. But a curious aspect to the story is that the bell on which the words had been inscribed was not the one cast by Thomas Lester in east London. It was not the original or 'authentic' Liberty Bell at all.

This fact introduces an important feature of the process of symbolisation, which cuts the material form of the bell loose from its moorings in the real. The Liberty Bell, we must bear in mind, is a symbolic form. It conveys the aspirational power of the will to liberty. And it is partly on account of its immaterial symbolic status that paradoxically such a high premium is placed upon the authenticity of the actual bell. This is why the object to this day attracts an air of devotion, as if the thing itself were capable of working some strange magic. In common with other objects that have their origin at the time of the revolution – clothes, pistols and muskets, even chairs – the bell has come to be venerated as a relic from the heroic past with the power to move one and encourage subscription to the great ideals which the Founding Fathers espoused. It is almost as if the subscription to political individualism in a secular state comes hand in hand with a need or desire for something in the realm of collective symbolism. Where once the church, certainly in its Catholic guise, provided many objects for collective veneration, now the state builds its authority on a set of commemorative rituals which create secular symbols out of material objects, or even individuals.

But the real history of the bell goes like this. When Lester's bell finally arrived in Philadelphia in August 1752 it was taken from Captain Budden's ship and set up in the State House yard. Its eventual home, the belfry up in the tower, had not yet been completed. But the townsfolk were impatient to test their new acquisition, so the bell was struck. Immediately 'the bell was cracked by a stroke of the clapper without any other violence'. The first plan was to send it back across the ocean and wait for a replacement, but it turned out that Budden already had a full load. At this point two local ironworkers stepped forward, John Pass and his friend John Stow, and offered to recast the bell even though they had never done such a thing before. They opined that something in the manufacture of the bell had made it 'too high and brittle' and that the addition of an ounce and a half of copper to the mix of ore would remedy the problem. The bell was duly smashed to pieces and then melted down, some further copper was then added before casting it afresh.

For a second time the bell was hung up in the yard and struck. No crack appeared but the sound was tinny and unimpressive. It is recorded that the two novice foundry men were 'so teased by the witticisms of the town' that they were stung into having a second attempt. Once again the metal was molten and then poured into the cast. This time the result was more successful, even though the sound of the bell was said to be rather unusual. It was this bell that was hung up in the completed bell tower in June of 1753.

For the first eighty or so years the bell was referred to as the 'Old State House Bell' or the 'Bell of the Revolution' or 'Old Independence Bell'; but in 1839 an anti-slavery pamphlet was published entitled 'The Liberty Bell' and this name was thereafter used to refer to the bell in Philadelphia. For a similar length of time the inscription on the bell was hardly remarked, but when Lippard's story appeared in 1847 the time was ripe for the final steps in the symbolic transformation of the material Pass and Stow had recast a century before. It is perhaps ironic that the year before Lippard's story was published the bell was struck for the last time.

From early on the bell had developed problems. A crack appeared and various attempts to close it (or even, curiously, widen it, as in 1846) were made. On this last occasion it was hoped that the bell might ring out in celebration of the day on which Washington had been born. But every attempt to heal the crack failed. And since 1846 the bell has been silent. But other bells have rung out, simulacra of the sound of the Liberty Bell have been heard on countless significant occasions, while the real bell, or rather the simulacrum of the *original* bell, has been seen, if not heard, by millions of Americans, either in its current home in Philadelphia or on one of its many journeys around the country.

For thirty years, between 1885 and 1915, the bell was frequently loaded onto a rail car and shipped around the United States. To New Orleans for the World's Industrial and Cotton Centennial in 1885; to Chicago for the World's Columbian Exposition in 1893; to Atlanta, Boston, Charleston, St Louis in the following years. On each occasion the tour would slowly wind its way through towns and cities, stopping along the way for the crowds to cheer, participate in parades and, on many occasions, kiss the bell which was hung from its original cross-beam, a single piece of hand-hewn black walnut.

The last time the bell was moved from its home town, Philadelphia, was in 1915 at the urging of 200,000 schoolchildren who expressed the wish that it be displayed at an exposition in San Francisco. But twenty-two years earlier in Chicago it had been decided to cast a 'new' Liberty Bell during the World's Fair so that once again its profound ring could be heard. This was not the first 'replacement' for the old bell whose crack prevented it from being struck. On the occasion of the centennial celebrations Henry Seybert, a wealthy merchant, paid for a new bell to be installed in the tower of Independence Hall. It weighed 13,000 pounds – a thousand for each of the thirteen colonies – and was made from the molten metal of four Civil War cannons. On 4 July 1876 at 12.01 a.m. it rang out for the first time. Yet another bell was cast, this time on the instruction of Queen Elizabeth II, and presented to the American people on the occasion

4. *A young child is held so as to touch the Liberty Bell on one of its journeys via rail car around the country during the late-nineteenth century. The crack, even at this resolution, is clearly visible.*

of the bicentenary of the republic. It was made in the same foundry as the original bell, the Whitechapel Foundry in London. And it bears the inscription 'Let Freedom Ring!' Today this bell hangs in a simple belfry that is part of the Independence Park Visitors Center in Philadelphia where, every day at 11.00 a.m. and 3.00 p.m. it is rung.

Holy relics have power on account of their presumed authenticity. Thus, even though these replicas and substitutes for the original bell exist and are struck in symbolic recognition of the mythic moment when the first bell rang out marking the Declaration on 4 July 1776, it is still the object itself which has the strange power of symbolisation. On New Year's Eve in 1976 the original bell, not the one cast in

Whitechapel but its recasting (twice) by John Stow and John Pass – was removed to a modern pavilion on the grassy mall below Independence Hall. A project to construct another home for it, begun in 2001, was completed in 2004. Visitors to this shrine – around one and a half million each year – are encouraged by the guides to touch its smooth surface and read the inscription which has inspired so many generations of Americans. When asked what they remember of their visit most people mention two things: that the bell is cracked and the name of what is now the state of Pennsylvania is spelt 'Pensylvania'. No one forgets the name by which the bell is known.

UNCLE SAM

Proudly marching at the head of countless Fourth of July parades is a man, or sometimes a boy, wearing a tailcoat, striped trousers and a beard. On his head there is a tall top hat that has been decorated with the Stars and Stripes. How did this figure – instantaneously recognisable as 'Uncle Sam' – become the symbolic figure for the nation? How did someone who would look more at home in a circus or on the stage become the person in whom all the passion and pride of patriotism would be invested?

It is commonly believed that Uncle Sam is hardly more than a comic-book invention, a relic of earlier times when periodicals frequently containing caricatures or cartoons were distributed across the United States. But in fact Uncle Sam was a real person, about whom we know quite a good deal. This is his story. He was born Samuel Wilson on 13 September 1766 in Menotomy, Massachusetts (now known as Arlington), the seventh child in a family of thirteen children, two of whom died in infancy. The family home was located in the triangle of land bounded by Massachusetts Avenue, Mystic Street and Russell Street. The title deed for this modest house indicates that a certain Robert Wilson purchased the property on 27 October 1665. It is not known where he hailed from, but it has been suggested that he had arrived in the United States from Scotland.

Samuel's father, Edward Wilson, married Lucy Francis of Medford on 23 November 1758. When Samuel was nine years old, in April 1775, news of the English action in the colonies was brought to Menotomy by Paul Revere on his now celebrated ride from Boston to Lexington. In 1780 the Wilson family sold up and moved to a hundred-acre farm near the hamlet of Mason, New Hampshire, just north of the Massachusetts line. Here Sam met his future wife, the daughter of Captain Benjamin Mann, a veteran of Bunker Hill and the proprietor of the local store and tavern. Nine years later Sam and his brother Ebenezer set out on foot, travelling west towards a town called Naderheyden, New York, about 150 miles distant. This village was well situated, seven miles north of Albany on the east side of the Hudson River. In January 1789 the freeholders in the village decided they needed a less cumbersome name and chose Troy, perfectly in keeping with the names of towns close by which were drawn from the classical tradition – such as Syracuse, Rome, Ithaca and Delphi. When the Wilson brothers arrived the village had just accepted this alteration in its nomenclature, and the new arrivals, Sam now twenty-two years of age and his brother Ebenezer twenty-seven, found work as brick makers. They were successful enough at this enterprise to form their own company making bricks and then in 1793 they decided to diversify by entering the meat-packing business. This involved the purchase of land on which to situate a slaughterhouse and a dock for loading sloops with barrels of beef and pork destined for points south down the Hudson. A large farm was also started to provide the meat for their expanding business, which went by the name of E & S Wilson.

It turned out that their choice of location, Troy, was a good one since it rapidly began to expand in the early years of the nineteenth century, as did its enterprises. This was partly fuelled by the fact that the US government bought 300 acres of land in Greenbush, New York, just south of Troy, where it established barracks for 6,000 soldiers. By 1812 when the war came, E & S Wilson had grown into a company substantial enough to bid for government contracts supplying barrelled meat to the army. In fact as early as 1805 the brothers had claimed that they were able to butcher and pack 150 head of cattle a day. Their bid was successful, as was Sam's application to become an inspector of beef and pork for the northern army. All this is a matter of historical record, but it hardly makes for a gripping story. For that we need to reach to another narrative form, to the legend that is Uncle Sam.

Here is how that legend got started. It appeared in the New York *Gazette* of 12 May 1830:

Immediately after the declaration of the last war with England, Elbert Anderson, of New York, a contractor, visited Troy on the Hudson, where was concentrated, and where he purchased, a large quantity of provisions – beef, pork etc. The inspectors of these articles at that place were Messrs. Ebenezer and Samuel Wilson. The latter gentleman (invariably known as 'Uncle Sam') generally superintended in person a large number of workmen, who, on this occasion, were employed in overhauling the provisions purchased by the contractor for the Army. The casks were marked E.A. – U.S. This work fell to the lot of a facetious fellow in the employ of Messrs. Wilson, who, on being asked by some of his fellow workmen the meaning of the mark (for the letters U.S. for United States, were almost entirely new to them) said that he did not know unless it meant Elbert Anderson and Uncle Sam – alluding exclusively then, to the said 'Uncle Sam' Wilson. The joke took among the workmen, passed currently and, 'Uncle Sam' himself being present, was occasionally rallied by them on the increasing extent of his possessions.

Very quickly thereafter around the town of Troy all government property – everything, from wagons to arms or payrolls – was referred to as belonging to 'Uncle Sam'. Although the legend did not at first travel that far away from the Hudson valley, the use of the term 'Uncle Sam' to refer to the government gradually gained ground in the popular literature of the time. Seventy or so years later, in 1917, one of Sam's great nephews, Lucius E. Wilson, who was by then eighty-one, noted that the usage had become ubiquitous. Remembering his youth he said: 'I was about eighteen when Uncle Sam passed away. He was the old original Uncle Sam that gave the name to the United States.'

What had happened in those intervening years was the transformation of a fact, a life, into a myth. Leaving behind the real person and his story based in lived experience the Uncle Sam legend became part of the symbolic capital of the nation. This is how it happened. Initially Sam was encountered most frequently in cartoon form. The first depiction was

5. One of the first images of Uncle Sam, suffering with flu and being
administered to by a gleeful President Andrew Jackson who is holding the
improbably large syringe.

published in 1832, in which a man swathed in an American
flag is seated and attended by doctors, one of whom is the
president, Andrew Jackson, and he is drawing blood from
the ailing man. The words 'Uncle Sam in Danger' appear at
the bottom – a comment on Jackson's proposal to close down
the Bank of the United States. This same ensemble appeared
in a subsequent print published five years later (illustration
5), again representing the failure of the banking system. But
it was not until the 1850s that the caricature now so firmly
associated with the symbolic personification of the nation
– an old man dressed in patriotic garb with a tall top hat –
began to appear. Two famous American cartoonists, Thomas
Nast and Joseph Keppler, are often credited with the addition of long whiskers to the character in the years following

the Civil War. But at this time Uncle Sam was in competition with another cartoon figure, 'Brother Jonathan', for the emblematic honour of representing the country. The British magazine *Punch* was firmly committed to this 'Jonathan', as were many French cartoonists of the time.

It was the Civil War, however, that brought together two important figures – Abraham Lincoln and the heretofore mythic representative of the nation – and melded them into a composite that has since come to be the stock imaginative presentation of Uncle Sam. It helped in this regard that *Punch* often dressed their cartoon figure of Lincoln in clothes that echoed the stars and stripes. And Lincoln's beard was, of course, instantly recognisable. Following the Civil War the melded figure of Lincoln and the previous 'Jonathan' or 'Sam' character was a common feature of periodicals and newspapers. And then in the 1870s Thomas Nast began using a cartoon sketch that would prove to be enduring: Uncle Sam, in his flag attire with tall top hat and long whiskers. One of the first was published in 1874 and captioned 'A foreign and poisonous weed', in which a farmer is about to dig up a mushroom labelled 'communism' (illustration 6). Uncle Sam stands behind the offending fungus looking down with a stern gaze. Nast's figure often seems to have very elongated legs (illustration 7), which may have entered the popular imagination and given birth to the more recent custom of putting him on stilts at the head of Fourth of July parades.

Nast never indicated his source for the cartoon, but it is often claimed that he drew inspiration from Dan Rice, the most famous clown in America during the mid nineteenth century. Rice had begun his career in the circus as a trick rider, but he subsequently developed an act with a trained

A FOREIGN AND POISONOUS WEED.
U. S. "That's right, Mr. GRANGER; I thought you would not have *that* in your *field.*"

6. *Uncle Sam looks on as Mr Granger weeds his field. His hoe carries a message on the blade: 'In our noble order there is no communism and no agrarianism'. Appearing at the foot of the cartoon are the words: 'That's right, Mr Granger; I thought you would not have* that *in your field'.*

7. *Uncle Sam has his trousers fitted alongside a banner announcing civil service reform.*

8. Flagg's iconic 1918 depiction of Uncle Sam helping recruitment for the war.

pig he called Lord Byron. By the 1850s he had settled on being a clown, styling himself 'America's favorite clown', and dressed in a Stars and Stripes coat with a blue leotard underneath. His trunks were red and white and he sported long whiskers and a top hat.

There have been variants since Nast's day. Perhaps one of the most popular in its time was Joseph Keppler's, which has Sam as a pot-bellied knockabout comic, recognisable from the music hall of the era. Others depict Sam in rather more sober habit but in 1916 *Leslie's Weekly* put an image on the cover of its 6 July issue which was to become the most famous depiction of all. The caption read 'What are you doing for preparedness?' and it caught the eye of someone in the War Department who subsequently asked its creator, James Montgomery Flagg, to adapt it for a poster to be used in the war effort. The commissioned image clearly makes reference to the portrayal of General Kitchener on a recruitment poster used in Britain earlier in the First World War, and more than four million copies were printed in 1917 and 1918 (illustration 8). For many Americans this *is* Uncle Sam, catching the viewer with his stern, beady eye. In a development that could not have been foreseen by Flagg, it is this image, perhaps, which fuels much of the unconscious association of government with surveillance and interference in citizens' private lives in the early twenty-first century. Uncle Sam, with his fixed stare and all-seeing eye.

To this day cartoons continue to make great use of the Uncle Sam figure, and his role in the popular culture of the nation has largely been determined by this form of visual representation. The common figure of speech by which the government is referred to as 'Uncle Sam' has also wielded its own power. But the most ubiquitous use of Uncle Sam in more recent times has been in promotional material. One of the first companies to use Uncle Sam as a means for making a sales pitch was the furniture oil manufacturer Berry Brothers, which placed advertisements for its product in many magazines in the early 1900s. The caption read: 'Uncle Sam supplying the world with Berry Brothers hard oil finish'. He has also been used to help sell tomatoes (the Wapato Fruit and Cold Storage Company), pianos (the Baldwin Piano Company), Cream of Wheat, Campbell's

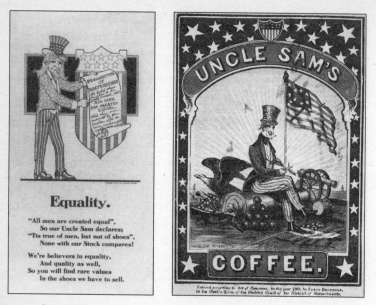

9 and 10. 'All men are created equal', so Uncle Sam declares, 'Tis true of men, but not of shoes'. To the left (9) an advertisement for a shoe company, to the right (10) a coffee supplier gets in on the act.

Soup, and Shoes (illustration 9). In fact almost anything that can be marketed and sold, coffee, say, is susceptible to the same endorsement (illustration 10).

It is likely that the real 'Uncle Sam' would have been surprised by his longevity as a symbol for the government of the nation. He might equally have been perturbed by the uses to which his 'image' has been put: in illustration 11 the use of Flagg's poster by a political group whose views can hardly be said to command widespread approval demonstrates both the symbolic power attached to the Uncle Sam icon and its adaptability. Another riff on the theme, issued in 1980 when Iran held US citizens

11. Flagg's image put to rather different political purposes. 12. A recent expression of Uncle Sam's patriotism during the 1980 Iranian hostage crisis.

hostage, was undoubtedly more sympathetically received (illustration 12). Whatever 'Uncle Sam' Wilson would have made of these images, the inhabitants of Troy, New York, set out to honour their most renowned former resident. A statue at Third and River Streets stands in commemoration of the life of Samuel Wilson, and to make sure it will never be forgotten that it was *this* solid citizen and successful entrepreneur who gave birth to the symbolic representation of the United States government, the good folk of the town approached the Senate in 1961. They were hoping to cast in stone, as it were, for all time the *fact* that Uncle Sam was once a real person made from flesh and blood. Their wish was granted when the Senate officially declared that Samuel Wilson of Troy, New York, was the inspiration or progenitor for Uncle Sam.

⧗

A flag, a bell and a cartoon character. Symbols which give meaning and expression to the rites of observance of the Fourth. In the cases of the first two, much of what we want to believe about them is based in the sense that stories make of the past. That sense is felt as a truth even if the foundations of the story lie in the playful enjoyment of fabulation. In the last, however, the facts we know to be accurate about a real person, Sam Wilson, hardly grab attention. He might as well have been a myth, a made-up character, since it is the symbol we want to believe in, not the man. But as symbols all three exist in a kind of historically insensitive ether, indifferent to the contingency of event. They are precisely symbolic on account of this strange power to resist alterations in meaning over time. Indeed, the use of these symbols in and around the rituals of the Fourth constitutes in part an act of preservation, maintaining something that has been inherited from the past. But the practice of this celebration could never be entirely symbolic. It lives and breathes in a different ether, the more knockabout world of events and actions. And so over time the meanings of the Fourth have been prey to the incidental even as its symbolic heart has continued to beat. The following chapter tracks those meanings.

4

THE MEANINGS OF THE FOURTH

A hundred years after Thomas Jefferson had given elo-
quent expression to the American mind the document we
now take to be *the* Declaration itself, the parchment with
the text carefully transcribed in legal hand which was
made on the instruction given by the Second Continental
Congress on 19 July 1776, found its way back to its 'birthplace', Philadelphia's Independence Hall, for the centennial
celebrations. It was ceremonially placed on the speaker's
stand before the expectant audience and read aloud by the
Virginian Richard Henry Lee, descendant of the man who
had first proposed 'that these United Colonies are, and of
right ought to be Free and Independent States' (illustration
13). For the previous thirty-five years it had been hung oppo-
site a window on an office wall in a government building in
Washington – the then recently built Patent Office – perhaps
not the optimal position for the long-term preservation of
one of the three foundational scriptures of the nation. Rather
curiously during these mid years of the nineteenth century
no one gave much thought at all to its darkening yellow
surface with the fading signatures at the bottom. Certainly
no one proposed to preserve or protect the document as an
object of near talismanic power.

The Declaration's most recent travels have been to the

13. *Richard Henry Lee reads from the Declaration to the celebrants at the Philadelphia centennial of the fourth.*

stage of a global rock concert, Live 8, held simultaneously in a number of locations worldwide on 2 July 2005 to raise consciousness about the plight of the peoples of the African continent. This event, organised by pop stars and hoping to build on the enormous success and importance of the Live Aid concerts held twenty years earlier, was watched by a global audience of millions. On the Philadelphia stage the actor Will Smith participated by introducing one of the acts, as did many personalities from the worlds of television and cinema in this and the other venues. On taking the stage he was accompanied by two Marines in uniform who positioned themselves either side of a display case containing the Declaration of Independence. Smith began his short stint as anchor for this segment of the show by first introducing the audience to the document. It was not made clear why the political let alone the entertainment objectives of the occasion were advanced by this gesture but in a curious way the mere presence of the parchment – introduced in a fashion which seemed to give the venerable document a sense of person, as if one were being introduced to an aged relative – produced its own mysterious and powerful eloquence. It was there as a reminder to the world-wide audience, many of whom were certainly ignorant of its history, perhaps even of the history of the foundation of the United States, that we have it within our power to initiate political acts that can change the world.

Between the mid nineteenth century and today the meanings of the Fourth have been interpreted in many ways, often determined by specific political agendas or coloured by important events, be they national or international. In fact the larger history of the nation can be seen – albeit in either a rather condensed or only outline form – in the changing focus given to the annual celebration of the nation's birth. What happened on that day, the words and actions of so many individuals in many different places, can be extracted from the archive that is the nation's history and help one take the temperature of the times. It is hardly surprising, for example, that in the years immediately following the War of Independence the rites of the Fourth were still tightly bound to the political and even emotional resonance of the declaratory act itself. And, of course, for as long as survivors from the generation of '76 were still able to attend Fourth celebrations the sense of connection to the events of July 1776 could be made palpable. But as the original event became more distant over time that connection had to be remade or reimagined if the rites of the

14. *Uncle Sam contributing to the war effort as 'fireworks' burst in the sky around him.*

Fourth were to continue to have similar significance for later generations. Such attempts at preserving the original meanings of cultural practices are not likely to succeed, of course, at least in the long term, since the proximate contexts of celebration provide an ever changing set of parameters for understanding the rituals and rites of the day. And these more localised and immediate concerns, crowding in upon observance of the Fourth, are most likely to grab attention, creating meanings for this generation, this moment in time. An image captured towards the end of the First World War, a significant moment in world history, wonderfully conveys the pressures of the contingent (illustration 14). We must also remember that each year the Fourth rolls around it has gathered yet one more encrustation to its rites of observance, adding to the stockpile which consists of the many histories of the Fourth.

There are many ways of sampling the variety of this quilted history. One is to look at what the president at any one time chose to do on the Fourth. Although it would be foolish to imagine that the actions of the president on the day are more symptomatic of the nation's mood than other activities we might wish to focus upon, they do, nevertheless, provide a window onto specific moments in the nation's history which can help us begin to assemble the meanings of the Fourth through time. The third president, for example, was the first to open his official home to the public on the Fourth, where he received guests from all walks of life. Most presidents since that time have made a point of attending public events of celebration, though not always in the capital, and to greater or lesser extents have made themselves physically accessible to the citizens of the republic. Eisenhower, however, throughout his two terms as president spent the day at Camp David and invariably played a round of golf. Is this fact too slender to take the weight of a more general observation about the 'comfort zone' of the 1950s in America, the Eisenhower years of corporate expansion as the country evolved into a mature superpower? Is it just a weird irony that in 1970, while President Nixon was meeting at the Western White House in San Clemente, California, to thrash out peace negotiations over Vietnam, on the other side of the country in the capital at 7.30 p.m. his tape-recorded Fourth of July message was played out of speakers along the Mall? Given the role that tape recorders were going to play in the demise of Nixon's presidency this little snapshot of the Fourth seems to be pregnant with the submerged meanings of contingent historical facts.

Less speculatively, we can gain an insight into the larger history of the nation from certain Fourth celebrations which happened to coincide with significant events. One of the decisive moments of the Civil War, for example, occurred on 4 July 1863, when the Confederate army surrendered at Vicksburg. Although President Lincoln had yet to hear the news of the successful military campaign on the day itself, or of the victory at Gettysburg which had been won the day before, when this information did get to him he rose to the occasion by giving a 'Fourth' address three days later, on 7 July. This speech was widely printed in newspapers across the country and can be read as a proleptic oration for the more renowned Gettysburg address of 17 November that year. Lincoln, who had not taken a public role in the actual day's celebrations three days before, spoke as if it *was* the Fourth. He began: 'Fellow-citizens: I am very glad to see you tonight. But yet I will not say thank you for this call. But I do most sincerely thank Almighty God for the occasion on which you have called. How long ago is it? Eighty odd years since, upon the Fourth of July, for the first time in the world, a union body of representatives was assembled to declare as a self-evident truth that all men were created equal.'

As Garry Wills so deftly points out in his book *Lincoln at Gettysburg*, the fifteenth president was the great illusionist of political rhetoric, presenting himself as a different person according to the audience he was addressing. So it is difficult to state categorically that he was for this or against that, and this applies as much to the subject of slavery as many other concerns of his presidency. If in saying that 'all men were created equal' he meant to indicate agreement with the emancipation of slaves he was giving a spin to the words taken from the preamble of the Declaration which would not have been acceptable to many delegates at the Second Continental Congress. For, as we know, the paragraph in Jefferson's draft concerning the iniquities of slavery was removed in the process of Congress's editing of his text. And even if this paragraph had remained in the text the sense then, in 1776, of who had a claim to equal rights would certainly not have coincided precisely with one way of reading Lincoln's agenda. In 1863 'all men' could for some public figures comprise the totality of the human race. In 1776 many more would have wavered before committing themselves to such a proposition. And some would have vociferously withheld their support for a political philosophy that did not discriminate between the differences of skin.

The most renowned Fourth oration on the topic of equality is Frederick Douglass's speech to the Rochester Ladies' Anti-Slavery Society on 5 July 1852 (the Fourth falling on a Sunday that year). This speech, commonly referred to by its most famous line 'What to the slave is the Fourth of July?', was published as a pamphlet and had very wide circulation. Douglass actually said, 'what to the American slave ...' and the omission of the qualifying adjective tells us something about the will to universalism that characterises observance of the rites of the Fourth. Notwithstanding such appeals to the transcendental truths embedded in the Declaration which are the staple fare of Fourth orations, Douglass's address was, of course, *punctual*. It helped maintain pressure to right what many then believed was a wrong in the foundation of the nation: its blindness to the status of citizens of African origin.

In the course of what to us would be a long speech – orations given on the Fourth up through the nineteenth century could last for at least one hour – Douglass made good use of what by then had become conventional tropes of Fourth oratory. But in his hands these rhetorical topoi are given an ideological twist, even a new lease of life, as he sets about his task of chastising the audience for continuing to uphold the inequities of racism. Early on, for example, he refers to the Fourth as 'the birthday of your National Independence' and, in case the point has yet to be heard fully, he adds 'and of your political freedom'. He has recourse to this use of the second person pronoun throughout the speech as he seeks to distinguish himself from his audience. Indeed, he explicitly makes the point that the nation contains two separate kinds of person. On the one hand there are those who were the descendants of the white colonists – the citizens comprising his audience – and on the other those who continued to be held under the yoke of slavery. 'The 4th of July is the first great fact of your nation's history', he says, once again assigning the significance of the day to a community of citizens which excludes the speaker. And then, having invoked this trope of origin, he reaches to an image that penetrates to the heart of his message: that fact is, he says, 'the very ring-bolt in the chain of your yet undeveloped destiny'.

With this image another habitual trope of Fourth oratory is introduced. This figure has its roots in Christian millennial rhetoric which gives expression to the future achievement of the promised land. This sense of a destiny, a perpetual future horizon, is a common feature of interpretations of the meaning of the Fourth. One can find it in Bill Clinton's speech of 4 July 1996, when he said: 'America is a work in progress'. The same trope is embedded in President Carter's sentiment, declared on the Fourth in 1977: 'the work of freedom can never be finished, for freedom is not a temple that is completed when the last stone is in place, but a living thing that each generation must create anew'. Once again the narrative grammar of the Fourth produces an account of the American Project which for many citizens is and has been liberating. It gives full weight to the conceptual invention that is the Constitution in its derivation of legitimacy from those who speak in its name or on its behalf: we the people. But, as the history of the nation shows, such derivation of power may not always lead to universal outcomes. If freedom is an unfinished project the end of the story has yet to be written.

Both Carter and Clinton spoke in rather elevated terms to the concerns of their era, to issues which today continue to concern us. Douglass, for his part, was addressing the pre-eminent issue of his own time in a language that would have been instantly evocative to his audience: 'I have said that the Declaration of Independence is the ring-bolt to the chain of your nation's destiny ...' In fact he had not claimed earlier that the Declaration was a 'ring-bolt' – the image is here being extended by proximity to its first use where 'the fact of the Fourth' was said to be this ring-bolt in the chain of destiny. But it was the Declaration he wanted his audience to call to mind. As a whole Douglass's speech shows how a small number of themes or common elements may be rearranged in order to speak more compellingly to the immediate context. Hundreds of Fourth orations make reference to the purported 'Declaration' in the sense of a speech act, or to the mythical signing of the document itself on that day. They nearly always include some words from the document (commonly either the preamble or the final few sentences, sometimes both) and often refer to previous explanations of their meaning, pointing up, for example, the rights and obligations of the citizen in a republican state. And many, very many, come to a conclusion by evoking the ultimate (future) realisation of the spirit of '76: the destiny of America. This common stock of rhetorical topoi constitutes a resource of extraordinary symbolic power and it may surprise us, living at a time when the technical arts of rhetoric and oratory are no longer taught in a formal way, that such a small palette can provide enough material for ringing countless changes on a perpetual theme.

Douglass, however, has a more specific agenda. At about ten minutes into the speech this becomes more apparent as he highlights his own position as a *representative* chosen to speak on this august occasion. For, whom does he represent? 'Fellow citizens' he starts off, 'pardon me, allow me to ask, why am I called upon to speak here today?' Given the room in which he was standing this can only be taken as a rhetorical question since his hosts were fully attuned to and in agreement with the tenor of his political agenda. Nevertheless, he makes the point assuredly: 'What have I, or those I represent, to do with your national independence? Are the great principles of political freedom and of natural justice, embodied in that Declaration of Independence, extended to us?' It does not matter that later historians and political theorists will question whether or not the Declaration does, in fact, propose something like a Lockean view of natural justice. Here, once again, the plasticity of the sentiments Jefferson so brilliantly distilled allows – even invites – generation after generation to find in the document its own version of 'political freedom' and 'natural justice'. And this is so even when such political goods are said to be timeless and universal. Having, one more time, marked out his exclusion from the lofty ideal of freedom espoused by the Declaration, Douglass turns the screw by cloaking his next question in the unmistakable garb of religious observance: 'and am I, therefore, called upon to bring our humble offering to the national altar, and to confess the benefits and express devout gratitude for the blessings resulting from your independence to us?' Moving to a crescendo in this section of his speech he draws on the familiar millennial imagery of the sun: 'The rich inheritance of justice, liberty, prosperity and independence, bequeathed by your fathers, is shared by you, not by me. The sunlight that brought life and healing to you, has brought stripes and death to me'. And then, once again, he hammers his point home: 'This Fourth of July is yours, not mine'.

Lest his audience fail to recognise the biblical dimension to his oration he next moves into direct quotation: 'By the rivers of Babylon, there we sat down. Yea! We wept when we remembered Zion. We hanged our harps upon willows …' and so on, culminating with an appeal: 'O Jerusalem, let my right hand not forget her cunning.' The same move, albeit routed through a very different historical context, was made by Harry S. Truman in his Fourth speech in 1945. Although on that occasion there was little to celebrate – the war in the Pacific was still a serious threat to the nation – the rhythms and cadences of the Christian liturgy that lie so deeply embedded in the psyche of America are audible in his speech. 'In this year of 1945', he began, 'we have pride in the combined might of this nation which has contributed signally to the defeat of the enemy in Europe. We have confidence that, under Providence, we soon may crush the enemy in the Pacific. We have humility for the guidance that has been given us of God in serving His will as leader of freedom for the world.'

It would be strange if the tenor of the times did not exert some kind of centrifugal force on the meanings associated with observance of the Fourth. Times of war inevitably raise the ghosts of 1776 and the ideals of the revolutionary generation. But they also put enormous pressure on the reinterpretation or reaffirmation of what might be claimed to be the founding creed of the nation. George W. Bush, for example, responding to the most traumatic experience of hostility to those ideals encountered since the Declaration was written, the events of 11 September 2001, spoke of the 'creed of freedom and equality' that underpins the founding of the nation in his Fourth address in 2002. 'This creed draws our friends to us', he said, speaking from the Courthouse Square in Ripley, West Virginia. 'It sets our enemies against us, and always inspires the best that is within us.' And in keeping with the habitual topoi for the occasion he had recourse to a religious metaphor: 'In this 226th year of our independence, we have seen that American patriotism is still a living faith'. Almost forty years earlier, as the country pursued a war far from its own borders, the faith Bush refers to was tested almost to breaking point in one constituency: the so called 'counter-culture' which so strenuously voiced its opposition to Vietnam. On the Fourth that year, 1968, anti-war demonstrators made Vice-President Hubert Humphrey's speech in Philadelphia difficult to listen to in a public manifestation of dissent from the leadership of the nation. And for many Americans of that generation the ideals and aspirations embodied in the founding Declaration were shown up in a new and far from favourable light by the prosecution of the war. It was precisely this animus which prompted Ron Kovic to write his memoir, which in 1989 was made into a film by Oliver Stone, entitled *Born on the Fourth of July*.

That film opens with a scene in which the military parade in a small-town celebration of the Fourth is shown to be formative for the young boy who will proudly grow up a patriot, ready and willing to give service to his country even while all those around him – his American schoolmates – evince little enthusiasm for enlisting in the fight against communism. Early on in the screenplay the sacrifice made by the Kovic character in signing up for the Marines is also shown to have repercussions in the family since his younger sibling takes a very different view of the wisdom of the war. But when the young Marine is wounded in action and heroically fights to save his damaged legs in a grim military hospital the realities of the war begin to surface. There is no money to fund sanitary conditions for convalescence. In fact the wounded are effectively marginalised, deprived of their citizenship. And so the Kovic character begins to alter his views and by the end of the film has become a vocal opponent of the war and the government which sent its young into battle.

Stone's movie does not speak for everyone of the Vietnam generation, nor does Kovic's book, but the simple and

effective message – encapsulated in the title – is fully embedded in the structure of celebration of the Fourth. What was
'born on the Fourth of July' is timeless, a set of ideals and
aspirations that may be knocked about by specific events,
reimagined or refocused, but inevitable as such contingency
may be, the obligation to diminish the power of immediate
concerns and contexts in order to cherish and preserve, to
pass on to future generations of Americans 'these truths …'
is shown to be the very essence of citizenship. No one can
argue with that as a founding creed. While some viewers may
take a very different position about the country's involve-
ment in Vietnam and the necessity of tackling those who
many judged to be mortal enemies of freedom and equality,
few would dissent from the account the film both explicitly
and implicitly gives of the obligations of citizens to honour
the credo of the Fourth.

An unfurled Stars and Stripes proudly ruffles in the wind,
the flag fixed to its mast, as is customary, on the left hand side.
Behind the flag a landscape stretches out to the horizon. It is
a scene of tranquil rural calm. A church occupies pride of
place in the small hamlet, painted white with a tall steeple.
A road slowly winds its way in serpentine fashion from the
foreground through to the rolling hills in the background.
Under the image of this bucolic paradise the words 'Land
of the Free' are printed, and below these words, in smaller
type, 'What price freedom before the election?' And under
these words, in parentheses, 'U.S. at War'.

So appeared the cover of *Time* magazine for 6 July 1942
(illustration 15). Following the bombing of Pearl Harbor
in 1941 a campaign was launched encouraging magazines
the length and breadth of the United States to include
the national flag on their cover for the issue published on

or around 4 July 1942. The idea was to flood the nation's news-stands and billboards with the patriotic message 'united we stand'. Almost three hundred magazines participated, from *Vogue* to the *New Yorker*, *US Steel News* to *Captain Marvel*. Paul MacNamara, a publicist working for Hearst Magazines, dreamt up the scheme, which was also backed by the Secretary of the Treasury at the time, Henry M. Morgenthau Jr, who was keen to raise more cash for the war effort through the 'Buy Bonds and Stamps' initiative.

Of course, each cover was designed with the target audience for the magazine in mind, but when one looks at them as a group it becomes possible to construct an image of America half-way through the twentieth century (illustrations 15–22). A country then committed to the Second World War and, in the aftermath of Pearl Harbor, facing a very real threat of attack and even invasion by a foreign power. So these images, published to coincide wherever possible with the day celebrating the 'nation's birthday', provide us with a powerful forensic tool for establishing some of the ways the Fourth has been used and represented. Although one cannot but be impressed by the ingenuity brought to the task by many of the designers of the magazines, taken as a whole it is less this spirit of invention that emerges and rather more a vivid image of how America, in 1942, pictured itself to itself. The anniversary (or thereabouts) of the nation provided an opportunity for both small niche market magazines, say *Flower Grower*, and national icons such as *Newsweek* to depict what, from their own corner of the pitch, seemed to them of significance for America's birthday.

Many were, of course, keenly aware of the war situation and the need to keep up the effort in supporting the Allied forces. *Boeing News* (illustration 16), for example, included

15

16

17

18

Eight covers from magazines published on or close to 4 July, 1942.

one of the traditional elements of the Fourth in the lower right-hand corner where the word 'fireworks' appears. Given that the military personnel pictured are loading bombs onto what we assume to be a Boeing bomber it is unclear as to whether the use of this word was intended to be playful or not. While *Infantry Journal* (illustration 17) was rather more appropriately sombre in regard to the ongoing war, its companion *Pacific Marine Review* was rather more positive, claiming that 'Ships will win the war!' while managing to include a more traditional up-beat, even celebratory, Fourth of July mood in the image of a ship being launched in the traditional manner. It would be difficult to envisage any outcome except a happy one from this particular presentation of a country at war.

It is, however, those magazines without any military connection whose covers create a patchwork of how America looked and felt to its citizens in 1942. The magazine *Theatre Arts* (illustration 18) had no particular need to make reference to a military theme, but it chose to depict a troupe of players entering an army camp in a motorcade that clearly nods towards the Fourth's tradition of the parade. Each truck carries props and contented-looking players who are busy learning lines from their scripts. The rhetoric of the image is disarming; it says 'Do not panic, we will prevail'. Above all it carries the impression of a young and inexperienced populace dealing with an unusual situation: war. A more serious note is struck by *Photoplay combined with Movie Mirror* (illustration 19), a journal aimed at the movie industry. This cover presented identity photographs of twelve movie actors who were currently serving the country, reminding readers of the gravity of the situation. Its strip line along the bottom announced 'How Clark Gable is Conquering

Loneliness', which one assumes was not a reference to his being marooned on a vessel somewhere in the Atlantic, but rather his efforts at keeping spirits up when so many of his colleagues and friends were doing service. In such a time one can forgive the rhetoric of heroism as displayed on the cover of *Look* (illustration 20). Here a lone soldier, standing on a promontory and looking out to sea, adopts the at-ease pose next to the flag run up an extremely tall flagpole. The words 'united we stand' take on particular resonance, implying that a lone soldier in a far-off and distant land is just as much a member of the collective as anyone else. This cover seems to be picturing the motto the nation adopted on its seal: *e pluribus unum.*

A rather more festive look is given to *Gourmet: The Magazine of Good Living* which does not allow its readership to forget that even in wartime the celebration of the Fourth ought to be graced with appropriately garlanded cookies and desserts in red, white and blue. But it is the covers of magazines such as *Outdoor Life* (illustration 21) which suggest that the rhythms and cadences of American life will prevail no matter what. Indeed, that such habits and customs are hardly touched by the war effort. And one cannot but admire the sheer bravado of *Capper's Farmer* (illustration 22) in its portrayal of the healthy smiling youth of the country making their own contribution by 'lickin' stamps.

This last image brings to the fore the significance of the Fourth in the modern calendar of family life and the place of children in it. For most of the latter half of the twentieth century it would be inconceivable to mark the anniversary of the 'birthday of the nation' without including children in some fashion in the celebrations. To some extent they have always been included as spectators: even in 1777 in

Philadelphia the parade and illuminations were enjoyed by those not yet old enough to be enlisted in the local militia or assume household responsibilities. But the primary or most prominent activities of the Fourth only slowly became aligned with those engaged in on other public holidays. It was not, for example, until the middle of the nineteenth century that entertainments such as balloon demonstrations or fairground attractions began to take on a predominant role in Fourth festivities. Even then the social and political meanings of a 'public holiday' were not, as now, so firmly embedded in the culture's promotion of the notion that time away from the workplace is best – and most morally defensible – spent within the enclave and embrace of the family. For the late-twentieth-century American workforce the number of days of 'enforced' holiday – those days designated as officially devoted to activities other than paid work – are far from numerous. Some, such as Christmas, maintain their significance as punctual religious rituals, but others such as Thanksgiving, which has its origins in a colonial Puritan observance of a day given over to worship, have been reoriented over time.

The Fourth, as we have seen, does have its feet in the clay of its colonial cultural origins and, on account of that, its connection to the religious observance of a 'day of rest' has not yet been completely erased. But inevitably over time the senses of celebration change as the years pass and the activities deemed appropriate for such occasions as public holidays alter. The promotion of competitions for eating the largest number of hot dogs, for example, might not have been approved of let alone dreamt up by the generation of '76. And although the grandchildren of the founding generation might have been willing to imagine the development of certain ball games as national obsessions even they would have been surprised by the prominence that sport has attained in contemporary American life. But they would have been perfectly happy with the idea that the Fourth be celebrated from within the family, marking the day by providing entertainments for children, incorporating them into parades and picnics and, perhaps above all else, sending the day off with spectacular displays of fireworks. So although the Fourth cannot properly be said to be a day of religious observance it does, nevertheless, embrace its celebrants within a doctrine that is held as sacred as any religious creed: independence.

Happier times produce more contented and certainly less contested celebrations. Illustration 23 presents an image of the morning breaking on 4 July 1876 – a happy, contented family raising the flag that 'has waved one hundred years'. The centennial was perhaps intended to be the most unifying moment in the nation's history of observance of the Fourth to date. All over the country orations and addresses were given – more than 420 are listed in the database compiled by James R. Heintze – which in their different ways honour the founders while, at the same time, look forward to the evolution of the country into a mature republic with considerable, even pre-eminent power in the brotherhood of nations. These encomia to the unity of the nation must be seen, however, in the light of the deep divisions which had . emerged in the republic between the fiftieth anniversary of the Declaration and the centenary. A civil war had almost destroyed the project of the Founding Fathers and the bitterness which resulted from that conflict can still, to this day, be seen in the proud traditions of various localities wherever they may be geographically situated across the continent of the Union. But on 4 July 1876 most were prepared to put to one side the animosity which had soured North–South relations and celebrate what one newspaper called 'the permanent establishment of civil and religious liberty'.

Notwithstanding the dampening of such partisan political loyalties, the centennial anniversary was not regarded universally as an occasion for unambiguous celebration. Some were keenly aware of the cost of mounting a big parade – perhaps on the model of the 'World Fair' which had been initiated in 1851 by Queen Victoria at the Hyde Park Crystal Palace – while others were disaffected enough to point out that the nation had little to celebrate. It could easily have transpired that the day would go down in history as a damp squib had it not been for the citizens of Philadelphia. Lacking leadership from the federal government, the residents of the 'birthplace' of independence took matters into their own hands by organising an International Centennial Exhibition. Four hundred and fifty acres in Fairmont Park were set aside to accommodate the fair. A private corporation began drawing up plans for the celebrations and the pavilions which were to house them. Most of the money and all the organisation was provided by local citizens. The federal government proved to be indifferent to the proposed jamboree, relenting only in March 1875, when it finally came up with a half-million dollar grant. Throughout 1875 and early 1876 the buildings took shape – the Main Hall was said to be the largest building in the world and the Machinery Hall housed the world's biggest engine. The Horticulture Hall, the smallest of the five principal exhibition halls, measured 380 by 193 feet and was made almost entirely out of iron and glass; it contained horticultural specimens from all over the world. The conservatory or main hall alone boasted full-grown sago, date and cocoa palms, orange and lemon trees, camphor, eucalyptus, guava, mahogany, India rubber, and banana trees. Plant specimens from the South Sea Islands jostled next to a collection of rare plants sent from a greenhouse in England; a collection of ferns said to be worth $10,000 had been contributed by a collector from Amboy, New Jersey. No one could be in any doubt that here, in the birthplace of the republic, was the largest exhibition of the planet's diversity ever mounted. Here one could witness the fruit of man's most advanced technologies. Here in America.

In spite of all this ingenuity and proud demonstration of the height to which the nation had risen in only a hundred years the population of the federation of states remained largely sceptical. Many opined that the entire project would become a white elephant, perhaps never even to open. Almost at the last hurdle the enterprise seemed to wobble as funds were lacking to complete the preparations; private donations were now exhausted. But in a close vote in Congress a bill was passed authorising a loan of one and a half million dollars. The show proved to be an enormous success with over 100,000 visitors a day crowding into the halls eager to see the marvels on display. In keeping with the ambitions of such 'world fairs' few would leave in any doubt about the superiority of the nation's achievements. Here could be seen the biggest exhibition of photographs ever mounted; 75,000 feet of wall space accommodated paintings from Europe and America. Machinery Hall, at 1,402 feet in length, covered an area of nearly thirteen acres. Objects manufactured from all manner of materials could be purchased – glassware depicting the Liberty Bell was one of the biggest sellers, but not far behind were glass renditions of the Declaration of Independence and of Betsy Ross making a flag.

23. *A family, complete with Afro-American servant, hoist the stars and stripes on the centennial.*

All this brio – appropriate for a nation eager to present a confident and forward-looking face to the world at large – ought to be seen in the context of the years preceding the centennial which had witnessed a marked indifference, even hostility, to the razzmatazz surrounding the Fourth. Indeed, by 1876 many citizens preferred to celebrate 'Decoration Day', the forerunner of Memorial Day, rather than the Fourth. Notwithstanding the deep divisions which emerged in America's sense of the nation around the issues which led to civil war, the deep seam of patriotism which runs through the observance of the Fourth from its first celebration to today could not be repressed entirely. So, as the nineteenth century drew to a close, the meanings of the Fourth began to be reoriented as the patriotic purpose of its traditions were focused explicitly at children, for whom the day became associated with fairground attractions. Their parents, however, were keen to use the day as a means of inculcating the rules and ethos of good citizenry, of making patriots of their charges. Allied to this was a similar innovation designed to bring together the celebration of the nation's birthday with the moment at which new citizens, immigrants to the country, took their first symbolic step as Americans.

The first move in what was to become a campaign to lobby Congress with proposals to change the name of the day was taken in 1915 in Kansas City. On the Fourth that year a number of new citizens took their first oath of allegiance on a day designated by the state officials as 'Americanization Day'. They had taken their lead from the Committee for Immigrants in America, which had been formed following the successful strike of mostly immigrant labour in Lawrence, Massachusetts in February 1912. This prompted a number of corporate heads to begin to think of ways in which their mostly foreign workforces might be better assimilated into American culture. So they first formed the Committee for Immigrants which then, in 1915, proposed the establishment of another group, the National Americanization Day Committee (NADC), whose purpose was to institute a day for 'a great nationalistic expression of unity and faith in America'. And so was born the

'Americanization movement'. July 4th seemed to be an appropriate day to be co-opted for this purpose, and since 1915 hundreds of thousands of new American citizens have been naturalised on the day that celebrates the birth of the nation. The largest number on any single occasion occurred during the bicentennial celebrations in 1976. And the honour of this distinction falls to Miami, where the beach Convention Center was converted into a federal courtroom in order to naturalise 7,241 persons.

If moments have a particular force in respect to the creation of the ongoing story of the nation, places have no less a power to construct the magical 'fit' between the past and affective relations to it. The iconic sites for the rites of the Fourth are easily identified: the State House in Philadelphia, now called Independence Hall, the sites of important military encounters – foremost among them Lexington and Concord – Faneuil Hall in Boston, scene of so many important meetings which led to independence. But perhaps the place held in greatest affection for many generations of Americans, partly because it opens a window onto the interior life of public office, turning the official into the familial, is the house the third president designed and built in his home state of Virginia. And since 1963 every year on 4 July new citizens have been welcomed into the embrace of the nation in a naturalisation ceremony held on its lawns. The speeches given on that occasion at Monticello also weave a miniaturised history of the more recent past of the nation and, like the orations of the nineteenth century which precede them, they help us make sense of the Fourth, shaping and interpreting its meanings.

In fact, Fourth orations were given from time to time on the steps in front of the portico at Monticello some decades before the tradition of hosting naturalisation ceremonies got started. That given by Harry S. Truman in 1947 is particularly resonant, coming as it did at the conclusion of a world war that many had feared would end in defeat for the Allied powers. On that occasion Truman spoke of Jefferson laying 'the foundation of an independent democracy' and his efforts to form the 'basis for a truly democratic government'. Themes which are, of course, firmly centred in the tradition of Fourth observance even if many of the signers of the Declaration would have had difficulty in subscribing to the notion of a 'truly democratic government'. But the precise context of his oration also gave a resonance to his remarks which may still be felt today. For Truman and his colleagues were keenly aware that the nation had now accrued responsibilities not only in regard to the citizens of the Union and the abstract principles enshrined in the foundation of the republic but also to those outside its borders where such principles had yet to become holy scripture.

'Two years ago', Truman notes, 'the United States and fifty other nations joined in signing a great Declaration of Independence', only this time, in 1945 at the conclusion to the most traumatic world war yet encountered, that declaration spoke not only for the people of America, it was also intended to speak for a genuine universal, for the peoples of the world. This declaration, Truman points out, is 'known as the Charter of the United Nations'. Reckoning that he ought to provide his reasons for signing up to this document, he explained that he had done so 'because we had learned, at staggering cost, that the nations of the world cannot live in peace and prosperity if, at the same time, they try to live in isolation'. And then he moved into the familiar rhetorical territory of the rites of the Fourth: 'We have learned that nations are interdependent, and that recognition of our dependence upon one another is essential to life, liberty, and the pursuit of happiness of all mankind.'

Since 1963 thousands of new citizens have sworn allegiance to the flag for the first time at Monticello on the Fourth in a celebration of its rites that has a very particular feel and flavour. Here, at the house built by the man responsible for most of the words in the Declaration of Independence, presidents, ambassadors, secretaries of state, leading entrepreneurs and chairmen of charitable institutions have given their own slant to what it means to become, to be, an American. Gerald Ford, speaking in the year of the bicentennial, claimed that 'there is still something wonderful about being an American'. He went on to say that, even if we cannot express it, 'we know what it is'. Addressing his audience of newly minted citizens he said: 'You know what it is or you would not be here today. Why not just call it patriotism?'

It would not be inaccurate to say that patriotism is so firmly embedded in the celebration of the Fourth that the significance of the day could hardly be intelligible without some understanding of what it means to be a patriot. Of course, the word 'patriot' has itself been subject to the immediate contexts in which it has been used: 'patriots' at the time of the revolution sought to distinguish themselves from loyalists, whereas later in the nation's history – once the republic was secure – the senses of patriotism had no need to be distinguished in this manner. Leaving aside the desiderata of party politics perhaps the most significant and enduring uses of the term bring it firmly into the orbit of what is sometimes thought of as the distinctiveness of the American experiment: its unfolding according to providence. Orators on the Fourth from the early nineteenth century onward made the connection between the Founding Fathers, those patriots who brought into existence the nation, and the will of God. 'It can surely be no disgrace', the Charleston orator Richard Furman declaimed on the Fourth in 1802, 'but a high honor to our patriots, to say "They acted in the cause of God" and that "He smiled on their endeavours"'. Indeed, throughout the nineteenth century Fourth orations returned again and again to the theme of the blessings bestowed upon the nation: God had arranged things so that Adams and Jefferson gave up their lives on the fiftieth anniversary of the Declaration, indeed, it was maintained that he continued to watch over the world's only republic, having in earlier times looked benignly upon the first settlers. Time after time comparisons of a biblical kind were entered into. America, it was claimed, was 'the modern Israel of the Lord', it had been delivered 'from a second Egypt'. Francis D. Quosh, speaking on the Fourth in 1820, described the heroes of the revolution as putting 'their only trust in Him, who never deserts the faithful', a God who 'as he once led his chosen people from the task masters of Egypt, was able to carry his American Israel through the waves and wilderness of revolution, and to place them in the Canaan of peace and independence'.

These sentiments were far from unusual or aberrant musings of overly portentous orators: many Americans subscribed to the thought that the prosperity of the nation and its continuation as a free republic was in the hands of the divine creator. What else could prevent such a political structure falling into the abuses history demonstrates were inevitable in all earlier attempts at republican government? And, like those miscreant peoples from biblical times, Americans would also find their situation deteriorating if they neglected their Christian duties and obligations. Christianity, observers at the altar of patriotism were told, was the best defence of American liberty. The Bible not only allowed one to espouse patriotic views, it required one to do so. This led to the inevitable conclusion that 'Jesus Christ was a patriot', as George Bethune put it in 1835.

It was not only preachers and Fourth orators who reinforced this story. The very first substantial history of the nation, George Bancroft's ten-volume *History of the United States from the Discovery of the American Continent*, claims that Providence transformed a wilderness into a nation. Providence, then, provided a way of not only understanding the formation of the nation and its prehistory – the era of the Pilgrim Fathers who were seeking refuge from religious persecution – but also the future trajectory of 'America' itself. Just as the Union was the only true free state, cut loose from the tyranny of kings and queens, so its divine calling would lead others into freedom.

It has often been noted that the revolutionaries' ideal of the republic inserted patriotism in the place of religious creed; some have suggested that patriotism became a new kind of religion. But the complex interlocking stories borrowing many narrative structures from Christian texts, which give a sense and shape to the observance of the Fourth as a significant moment in the founding of the nation, create something more potent than a kind of 'secular religion'. For what the rites of the Fourth set loose into the republic is the potential to achieve, one day, the ideals embedded in a few well-chosen words which constitute, precisely, a *declaration*. They give notice to an intention. These words allow one to *perform*, through the act of speech, one's commitment to an ideal of liberty. As William T. Barry noted of the Fourth, a 'day consecrated to *freedom*', millions of Americans 'now assemble at the Temple of Liberty, and perform their worship at her shrine; and so long as her *genius* presides over and controuls [sic] the destinies of the Republic, this anniversary will be distinguished with peculiar joy and grandeur'.

While many, if not most, citizens have been content to sign up to the – albeit symbolically mobile – rituals of the Fourth and to assent to its most publicly available meanings, it should be remembered that for some the lofty ideals of the Declaration have never been delivered upon. It is for this reason that many 'alternative' declarations have been proposed. Perhaps the tradition that runs deepest in this vein of political dissent has been developed within the context of working men's and women's associations, within the history of American labour. Not all of these 'declarations' have been issued on the Fourth itself – the first, for example, appeared in December 1829 when George Henry Evans published his 'Working Men's Declaration of Independence' in the *Working Man's Advocate*. Following the text of the Declaration – 'we hold these truths to be self-evident ...' – Evans wrote that to secure these rights 'against the undue influence of other classes of society, prudence, as well as the claims of self-defense, dictates the necessity of the organization of a party, who shall, by their representatives, prevent dangerous combinations to subvert these indefeasible and fundamental privileges'. A 'declaration of the rights of the Trades' Union of Boston and Vicinity' was made in June 1834, the 'Anti-Renters' Declaration of Independence' was issued on 4 July 1839 and others in a similar vein were made right up to 4 July 1902, when the 'Working Class Declaration of Independence' appeared. These 'interpretations' of the Fourth's meanings share a concern for the politics of labour and seek to promote a sense of the unfinished project announced by the original document.

On the occasion of the centennial celebrations the National Woman Suffrage Association hoped to expose the government's poor record in respect to universal rights by reading a declaration at the official Fourth party held at the Exposition site in Philadelphia. They were denied access to the centennial park but the document, containing 'articles of impeachment' against the government, was read aloud by Susan B. Anthony to a large crowd outside Independence Hall on 4 July 1876. 'The history of our country the past hundred years', it claimed, 'has been a series of assumptions and usurpations of power over woman, in direct opposition to the principles of just government'. There followed a number of detailed descriptions of aspects of American legislation where discrimination against women was practised and upheld. Here, as with the various declarations made by groups seeking to protect and enhance the rights of working people, the meaning of the Fourth is derived in part from an ironic take on the realisation of the ideals declared in 1776. Thus, when the bicentennial came around, a group styling itself the People's Bicentennial Commission issued a document – the 'Declaration of Economic Independence' – that could almost be read as a parody of the original. Although there can be no doubting the seriousness of the political aims and objectives of this group of dissenters, the close adoption of the Second Continental Congress's text today reads like a script for an alternative comedy sketch. 'When in the course of human events', it begins in emulation, 'it becomes necessary for one people to dissolve the economic bonds which have tied them to another ...' And, continuing in the same vein: 'that to secure these rights, economic institutions are instituted among people ...', 'it is the right of the people ... to institute a new economic system ... ', 'prudence ... will dictate that economic systems long established ...', and so on. This perhaps demonstrates that the standard meanings of the Fourth are so deeply embedded in the unconscious of the nation that when quite legitimate political dissent from established government is garbed in words echoing the founding text its effect is counter-productive. At least counter to the aims of the People's Bicentennial Commission. If the contexts of the Fourth shine new light on the stories the nation lives by it remains the case that the words of the text itself lay too deep in the foundation of the American psyche to be wrested into new configurations without parody being the result.

The shape and character of Fourth celebrations has always reflected to some extent the wider political, social and economic situation of the time. It is hardly surprising, for example, that the years of the Great Depression were not enlivened by extravagant pageants and costly banquets. And the campaign to make the sale of fireworks illegal, which once again reared its head in 1937 when the National Fire Protection Association attempted to persuade all state legislatures to ban both the sale and use of fireworks, inevitably cast a pall over the traditional way of concluding celebrations on the Fourth. By 1953 twenty-eight states had banned all private use of fireworks and a further fourteen had strict regulations about the size and scope of private firework displays.

In the late twentieth century and early twenty-first the Fourth has become firmly tied to the 'backyard' tradition of celebration which began to develop in the 1950s. Large-scale public festivities – communal banquets, orations, parades of the great and good – were gradually supplanted by the family get-together. A charcoal grill and hamburger were more likely to feature in most Fourth celebrations than a speech on the spirit of '76. And where parades are still mounted they more often than not have very local flavours, giving pre-eminence to some event or institution which provides the context for a public celebration. In the era of mass communication the means for creating and promoting a sense of national identity – television, radio and the internet – have firmly replaced earlier forms such as print or the public address. Most people today will hear the words of the Declaration read aloud on the Fourth only if they turn on their televisions. To some extent this represents a significant break with the history of Fourth observance, a reimagining of the significance (or insignificance) of the founding moment. And for some this might suggest that any attempts to recover that history are bound to fall prey to the dynamics of nostalgia, of painting a rosy past for the purposes of the contingencies of the present. There are, however, continuities which drive deep into the bedrock of the nation's imagination.

One of those continuities, a feature of how the Fourth has been understood since the nineteenth century, is still pretty legible today: the use of the story of the Fourth as a primer for educating children into the first steps of citizenship. It is remarkable that so many books, from the late nineteenth century onwards, designed to help teach reading skills make use of the Fourth story. A survey of those books and others written for young children able to read on their own account demonstrates that the predominant meaning of the Fourth disseminated through this literature is its punctuality as the 'birthday' of the nation. In book after book – with titles such as *Doodle Dandy! The Complete Book of Independence Day Words* or *Give Me Liberty: The Story of the Declaration of Independence* – one encounters the familiar stories of the nation's founding. A typical example can be found in a book which seeks to explain the rationale behind all the public days of celebration observed in contemporary America, fittingly entitled *America Celebrates*. In the chapter devoted to Independence Day a short piece by Pamela Kennedy gives a particularly vivid account of the deep connection between childhood and the Fourth for contemporary America. She writes: 'Independence Day is about a lot more than freedom from Mother England. For me, it has as much to do with my freedom to be young again, to do silly things, and to enjoy simple pleasures that America has to offer.' And she goes on to characterise some of those 'silly' things that many will recognise, in spirit if not to the letter. The 'World Famous Precision Mower Drill Team', for example, which comprised twenty men dressed in trench coats and fedoras marching in columns, each pushing a lawn mower. Or the 'Largest Kazoo Marching Band in the Entire U. S. of A.', which she witnessed in Milwaukee. These examples catch the flavour of countless contemporary Fourth diversions and Kennedy sees it as an almost universal desire on the part of adults across the nation to 'drop the mantle of sophistication and get down to serious silliness on the Fourth'. As she remarks, the day has to do with 'remembering a time when I couldn't see moon dust up close or fly faster than the speed of sound. In short, I can be a kid again on the Fourth of July.' It is unlikely that Kennedy speaks for all adult Americans or that her views have very wide circulation; but the words of President Gerald Ford make a far greater claim for conveying something of the deep connection between current practices of

Fourth celebration and childhood. On the eve of the bicentennial celebration in 1976 he said, 'I knew what happiness was when I was a boy. It was the Fourth of July.'

How did the rites of the Fourth become so bound up with the meanings of the Declaration itself? As everyone knows – or believes – the day is set aside to celebrate the signing of the Declaration. And that act is taken to signify the birth of the nation. Why, in the current era when the pomp and ritual of the day have been largely consigned to history, now replaced by the familial setting of the backyard or the school house, does the celebration of the Fourth transcend region and locality and reach outward to the larger context of state or nation? In answering these questions we need to consider the ways in which the three 'founding' documents of the nation – the Declaration, the Bill of Rights and the Constitution – have become, in the words of historian Pauline Maier, 'American Scripture'. As she wonderfully evokes the conditions in which these documents are now kept, 'encased in massive, bronze-framed, bulletproof glass containers filled with inert helium "to displace damaging oxygen", and with water vapor to keep the parchment from getting brittle', it becomes clearer and clearer that they are now venerated as holy relics. Again, as Maier painstakingly demonstrates, the evolution of the attitude taken to the Declaration is intimately tied to the different ways in which the history, or better still the ongoing story of the nation, is told.

For what characterises contemporary observance of the Fourth can once again be conveyed by one word: independence. And, perhaps as importantly to the times we now live in, the notion that it might be desirable to 'declare' this independence seems vital to the senses of being American.

Independence is so strongly associated with the Fourth in contemporary life that the Declaration's meanings seem to have been distilled into a very modern take on the idea of citizenship and the notion of the individual on which it stands. Independence is synonymous with autonomy, the sanctity of the individual. No longer an expression of common beliefs and ideals, the Declaration today seems more like a performative act which by its very enunciation enacts an individuated independence. But this, as the final chapter sets out to demonstrate, is merely yet one more variation on a theme produced by the narrative grammar that beats deep in the heart of the Fourth.

5

CELEBRATING INDEPENDENCE

All day the temperature had barely moved below 100 degrees. The local sharps had made a killing selling fifty-cent bags of ice for five dollars a throw. And now, as the hour neared midnight, the guy with the bandanna and the guitar he played as naturally as if it had been an extra limb was surfing the stretched notes, carried onward and inward towards the clear light he felt was home. Eyes tight shut. Lips slightly parted. Kissing the fetid air that was his breath. Jimi Hendrix, who would be found dead ten weeks later in London, his body quietened for the last time by the junk that had sustained him, was at this moment supposed to give Alex Cooley a signal. Cooley needed a sign from the stage in order to time the commencement of the fireworks. It had been agreed that on the stroke of midnight, 4 July 1970, Hendrix was to break into 'The Star-spangled Banner' and, like millions of citizens across the country, wish America 'happy birthday'.

On that day the US secretary of state, William P. Rogers, had been in Saigon attempting to negotiate a settlement to the increasingly unpopular war in Vietnam. A British air-liner crashed into a mountain in Spain, killing 105 passengers. Bob Hope, Jack Benny and the Reverend Billy Graham, among others, had stood in front of thousands of citizens in

Washington, DC earlier in the day to 'honor America'. And Hendrix had lost the plot.

Alex Cooley, a promoter from Atlanta, had organised the first Atlanta International Pop Festival the year before. In its second year, just one year on from Woodstock, it had been promoted as the natural successor to that gorgeous flowering of the counter-culture. It was billed as 'three days of peace, love and music'. The Allman Brothers came to play, as did BB King, Ravi Shankar, Jethro Tull and Ten Years After. And, topping the bill on 4 July, the counter-culture icon of the moment, Jimi Hendrix unfurled his unique quilting of rock, the blues and Afro-American oppression, a musical offering for the 500,000 supplicants who came to witness his devotions. Tickets had been priced at $14.

'It was our Woodstock', R. Palmer Marsh said. He had driven from Atlanta to the tiny central Georgia town of Byron with friends. The traffic had been backed up the entire ninety miles from the state capital. 'Most of us here didn't go to New York in '69, and Byron brought it south to us. It was a phenomenon, a once-in-a-lifetime event. I didn't really go for the music. The scene was the attraction.' The local law enforcement had been expecting maybe 100,000, but 'there were so darn many of 'em, they ran the alligators and the water moccasins right out of the Echeconnee Creek', claimed the police chief, James Barbour. So, for three days, 500,000 people put up tents in a pecan grove next to the Middle Georgia Raceway. And they had a festival.

Not everyone found it to their taste. Mary Marsh, an artist in the region, had just graduated from high school. She went with a date, perhaps ill prepared for the peace, love and music she was to encounter. When her man pointed to a naked guy in the process of painting himself with the contents of a few cans of Campbell's soup she chose to look away. The heat was unremitting. 'Nobody was selling Coca-Colas', she said, 'only Kool-Aid with LSD in it.' A number of tents within the festival site were declared 'OD' tents. Hundreds of festival-goers had availed themselves of the services of volunteer doctors who attempted to bring solace to those coming down from bad trips. And there, on stage in the wet, hot night air was the cheerleader for America's refuseniks. Earlier in the summer the forces of law and order had beaten up those who chose to make their disaffection with the administration's policies public. Kent State was still a gaping wound in the counter-culture's psyche. And Hendrix, smashing into 'All Along the Watchtower', 'Hey Joe', 'Voodoo Chile', and 'Freedom', was providing the soundtrack. Perhaps it was inevitable that the song he was lost in, the soaring trip of a solo he couldn't, or didn't want to conclude was 'Stone Free'. So he fluffed his lines and Cooley had to let off his fireworks sometime into Hendrix's irreverent rendition of the national anthem.

As one would expect, the traditions of celebrating the Fourth have evolved over time. In the first half of the nineteenth century the day was suffused with a distinct air of veneration as the palpable sense of connection to the Founding Fathers and the founding moment was still available. Often things were arranged to encourage if not enhance the feeling of being connected to an 'epochal' moment. Thus in 1821 John Quincy Adams, the son of one of the signers and himself a future president, read from an original copy of the Declaration at a ceremony held in the Capitol. Thirteen years later, in 1834, a man who was at Lexington and Bunker Hill attended the ceremony in New Haven, Connecticut, wearing the coat he had worn in 1775 when the English had opened fire. Five years after that a student at a Sabbath school in Norwich, Connecticut, read excerpts from the Declaration wearing 'the identical cap' worn by William Williams, a delegate from that state, who had signed the Declaration wearing the said cap.

In fact for the first fifty or so years following the original declaration there seemed to be a special power attached to any human connection to the original moment. In the early years those who had signed the document – no matter that they had not actually signed it on the 4th – were wheeled out to take leading roles in the celebrations wherever they may have been held. By 1828 only one such person remained alive, Charles Carroll, and he duly participated in the Baltimore celebrations that year. But as the original signers became thin on the ground other, less immediate, connections seemed to emanate similar powers of authenticity. On the fiftieth anniversary, for example, Major John Handy read the declaration in Newport, Rhode Island, 'on the identical spot which he did 50 years ago' and he was accompanied by Isaac Barker of neighbouring Middeltown, 'who was at his side in the same place fifty years before'.

To some extent this reverence for anything making a claim to the punctuality of the event, to authenticity in a very palpable sense, was almost an ethical desideratum. It encouraged an attitude and instilled in the celebrant a feeling of almost religious awe. Even Jefferson – proud architect of Virginia's separation of church and government – was not immune to this strange power of reverence. It can be said that in some sense, towards the end of his life, he promoted it. Writing in a late letter to his granddaughter, Ellen Wayles Randolph, about the 'plain, neat, convenient' writing desk on which he had written the draft of the Declaration, he muses that at some future date this object might be 'carried in the procession of our nation's birthday, as the relics of saints are in those of the church'. Perhaps we should not be surprised at the old man's wish to see the spirit of '76 honoured, even rekindled; as the last letter he wrote puts it: 'let the annual return of this day forever refresh our recollections of these rights, and an undiminished devotion to them'. Certainly early nineteenth-century celebrants of the Fourth would have recognised the tone of religiosity which crept into Jefferson's attempts at myth making. The hardly veiled gestures towards the veneration of iconic objects might, however, strike a Catholic note which is surprising. Indeed, the continuous pressure in the stories of observance of the Fourth to found a myth of incarnation sits awkwardly within the standard conception of the puritan basis for the society in which the revolutionaries came into maturity. Is this a case of making good use of whatever one can in the creation of the belief structures which are to give sense to the founding and history of the nation, or is there some compelling attraction to idolatry deep in the founders' mythopoeia?

As the shadow of the first Fourth of July lengthened, the physical links to that day inevitably began to weaken. But later eras have not been unadventurous in their attempts to re-forge the bonds of connection and authenticity. What strange aura or frisson of excitement was experienced by the 10,000 people who crammed into Independence Hall in 1853, all of whom attempted to sit (thankfully not all at once) in the chair occupied by John Hancock, the president of the Second Continental Congress? What particular privilege might it have been to have heard the 'real' Liberty Bell ring? What were the celebrants packed into the Kennedy Center in Washington, DC on the Fourth in 1974 thinking as they listened to a re-enactment of Frederick Douglass's oration 'What to the Slave is the Fourth of July'?

In the attempt to make that connection both resonate with the past and speak to the present the accidents of history itself have often been enlisted. So, for example, one of the very first sound films ever made was of Calvin Coolidge giving his Fourth of July speech in 1920 before he had been nominated to run for vice-president. In 1941 the day was marked by Chief Justice Harland Fiske Stone leading the nation in a live radio broadcast of the 'Pledge of Allegiance' from Estes Park, Colorado. In 1945 the Stars and Stripes was hoisted over Berlin's Adolf Hitler Barracks in a formal 4 July ceremony and a 48-gun salute was sounded. In 1992 the seven astronauts aboard the space shuttle *Columbia* unfurled the Stars and Stripes and sang 'Happy Birthday, America' from space. In 2003 US troops celebrated the Fourth with a cookout at Saddam Hussein's hometown palace, while in 2004 the cornerstone of the Freedom Tower was laid on the former site of the World Trade Center.

It is true that local communities no longer divide into warring party factions holding rival Fourth celebrations, as early nineteenth-century Bostonians did. Orations and celebratory odes penned by local personalities no longer feature in the vast majority of town or city parades. Most Americans will spend their day away from work within the context of the family, perhaps in a park with a picnic, or by the side of a lake, or just in the home's backyard. But the day continues to have significance within the calendar of national events. The president will attend a public occasion – health or more urgent matters permitting – at which a parade, almost certainly military in some degree, will take place. And a speech will be made. Although the gravitational pull of the founding moment is no longer felt, the punctuality of the day continues to be honoured. Thus many local organisers of the celebrations will have an eye out for something that might give a particular, singular flavour to the day – say the opening of a new bridge, or the dedication of a public monument. In Louisville, Kentucky, a new Waterfront Park was dedicated on the Fourth in 1999; Rockford, Illinois, did likewise to a granite war memorial in Veterans Park the same year, and examples like these could be multiplied a thousandfold. And then sometimes, pleasingly, events seem to conspire miraculously to honour the day, as in 1997 when the spacecraft *Pathfinder* landed on Mars.

Every year there are hundreds of such punctual moments which may have only very local association or significance. But notwithstanding these more intimate meanings there is a common feature to them all: they take place on the same day which by rite and history commemorates one thing, America's birthday. Each and every year these celebrations, no matter what their specific focus might be, participate in the ongoing making of the republic. They add another strand to the fabric of the story that is the Fourth of July. And in doing so they bind each celebrant into the larger history of the nation. Even if current modes of public political behaviour are less demonstrative or collective than they were in the nineteenth century, there nevertheless remains a strong sense of adherence to the principle given voice by the single most important word of the document that, sealed under glass in a vacuum, ought now to be preserved for ever: independence.

This word conveys both the legacy of the generation of '76 as well as the prospective ideal each citizen commits to in celebrating the declaratory act of founding. An independence which may be located in or claimed by the unique individual but whose guarantor is the collective. That ideal comes clothed in universalism – although George W. Bush was far from the first person to say it, the words he spoke on 4 July 2003 capture a very significant feature of the political act that is the ongoing observance of the Fourth. Speaking at the United States Air Force Museum in Dayton, Ohio, he said, 'The Declaration of Independence holds a promise for all mankind.' And then in explaining why this is so he adverted to the proprietorial rights that come bound up in the declaratory act: 'Because Americans believe that freedom is unalienable right, we value the freedom of every nation.'

Perhaps the most remarkable feature of the Fourth is its capacity to withstand being wrested into many conceivable contexts. Even when that context, as in the scene with which this chapter began, may be hostile to anything like a sense of veneration or good manners in the face of the symbols held dear to the traditions we have been tracking. The great strength of the rituals of the Fourth lies in the capaciousness of its symbols. But even if specific contexts may inflect the core meanings of those rites in new and different ways, something immutable remains deep in the heart of their observance. For each and every time the Fourth rolls around in a kind of Groundhog Day recursion a declaration is made that is founded on an architecture of belief that may well endure to the end of time. And the lineaments of that architecture are conveyed in the phrase Jefferson so brilliantly captured: 'we hold these truths to be self-evident'.

Philosophically speaking the notion of a truth having a

quality of 'self-evidence' is not particularly easy to grasp. Those who eventually put their signature to the document were mindful of this, introducing the statement of their beliefs '*we* hold these truths …', thereby indicating they were aware they may have, at least initially, seemed eccentric. Or held views requiring careful justification. But the conceptual muscularity of this formulation, what gives it such enduring power, is not the part about self-evidence. It is the performative act of declaring a commonly held architecture of belief.

If we compare Jefferson's first thoughts for this phrase – he wrote 'truths held to be sacred and undeniable' – to the phrase millions have committed to heart – 'we hold these truths to be self-evident' – we can see how this revisionary stroke of genius creates a new kind of belief structure. To say that something 'is held' to be sacred is to subscribe to a theological creed which provides the architecture for one's belief system. And what may be sacred to one theology, say a cow, may well not be so to another. But in saying 'we hold' the speaker is indicating something radically different. Far from subscribing to a theology or a metaphysics, the speaker is deriving the imprimatur to the truths that are self-evident from the act of claiming, in common with others included in the 'we', that 'we hold'. In the very declaratory act of saying 'we hold these truths' such truths are in and by that performance given the necessary support to enable the speaker to claim that she or he believes them to be self-evident. Consequently the basis for the belief is not a metaphysics but what might be called an *apodictic declaratory act*. And it is this act which creates a new architecture of belief. Just as government in the new political system that is the first modern republic is derived from 'we the people' governed, so the belief in the truths that are self-evident is derived from the declaratory act of stating that 'we hold'. It is a fundamentally new conceptual departure, the most daring innovation in the philosophy of government since Machiavelli's *The Prince*. Perhaps – it is devoutly to be wished, since humankind has not bettered it – the most enduring conceptualisation of the authority and legitimacy of government there will ever be. The extraordinary gift of those who have come to be called the Founding Fathers. America's signature.

Each year on 4 July Americans celebrate the birthday of their nation. The rites and rituals of the day have undergone changes of focus and alterations in precise content since the first celebrations in 1777. Although the symbols which continue to play a significant role in the practice and under-standing of those rituals are less prey to the forces of change, they too, like the reverence in which the Stars and Stripes is held, inevitably come under pressure as the nation evolves. But one thing remains unchanging and is unchangeable: the power of being included within the 'we'. Both Adams and Jefferson, in their own ways, recognised this and wished to make it clear that what would become their legacy, the legacy of the generation of '76, is also loaded with a burden of responsibility. For the we who give their consent give it on behalf of certain principles.

The story of the Fourth of July presents a supreme fiction. That the nation came into being on a particular day in 1776. It does not matter in terms of the coherence of the story whether or not this has any basis in fact. It does not matter insofar as one subscribes to this story that nations, complex geopolitical organisms, are never founded at a single stroke. For in telling this story something fundamental and very significant occurs: the declaration of a new kind of belief structure. *We* have it in our power to determine what shall be taken to be a self-evident truth. Each and every Fourth, as if for the first time, a new architecture of belief is both celebrated and instantiated in the many speaking as one. And in that collectively imagined common tongue 'America' by simple force of a declaration is founded. In celebrating independence each Fourth may it also be remembered that the birthday of the nation, the declaratory act that founds America, created and continues to create an architecture of belief which, for both good and ill, has power to change the world.

FURTHER READING

GENERAL

The research for this book would have been far more difficult without the help of the extraordinary database compiled by James R. Heintze, *Fourth of July Celebrations Database*, accessible online at http://gurukul.american.edu/heintze/fourth.htm.

Two books on the subject of the Fourth have also aided my research significantly: Diana Karter Appelbaum, *The Glorious Fourth: an American Holiday, An American History* (New York, 1989); and Len Travers, *Celebrating the Fourth: Independence Day and the Rites of Nationalism in the Early Republic* (Amherst, 1997). An unpublished PhD, R. P. Hay, 'Freedom's Jubilee: One Hundred Years of the Fourth', submitted to the University of Kentucky in 1967, provides a good amount of material for both of these more recent books and has also been extremely helpful for this study.

CHAPTER 1

The various myths surrounding the Fourth have been the object of scholarly study from time to time. The earliest of substance is Charles Warren, 'Fourth of July Myths', *William and Mary Quarterly*, 3rd series, 2 (1945). Less scholarly accounts are legion; see, for example, Cornel Lengyel, *Four Days in July* (New York, 1958); and Donald Barr Chidsey, *July 4th, 1776: The Dramatic Story of the First Four Days of July, 1776* (New York, 1958).

The literature on the Declaration of Independence is now very substantial. The book which can be said to have originated this scholarship and to which my own understanding of the process of making the Declaration is indebted is Carl Becker, *The Declaration of Independence: A Study in the History of Political Ideas* (New York, 1922). This work was made possible by John Hazelton, *The Declaration of Independence: Its History* (New York, 1906). Dumas Malone was the first scholar to put into general circulation the story of the Declaration's genesis, see his *The Story of the Declaration of Independence* (New York, 1954). More recently Pauline Maier's thorough and readable *American Scripture: How America Declared its Independence from Britain* (London, 1999) has been invaluable for my own project. Two further books of outstanding interest are Garry Wills, *Inventing America: Jefferson's Declaration of Independence* (New York, 1978); and Jay Fliegelman, *Declaring Independence: Jefferson, Natural Language, and the Culture of Performance* (Stanford, CA, 1993).

Scholars have been well served by exacting editions of many colonial- and revolutionary-era documents. In particular the *Journals of the Continental Congress, 1774–1789*, ed. Worthing Chauncey Ford (Washington, DC, 1904–6); the *Letters of Delegates to Congress, 1774–1789*, ed. by Paul H. Smith (Washington, DC, 1976–9); the *Letters of Members of the Continental Congress*, ed. by Edmund C. Burnett (Washington, DC, 1921–3); and *A Decent Respect to the Opinions of Mankind: Congressional State Papers, 1774–1776*, ed. James H. Hutson (Washington, DC, 1975), have all been crucial resources.

For an account of the Declaration as a physical document see Verner Clapp, 'The Declaration of Independence: A Case Study in Preservation', *Special Libraries*, 42 (December 1971). The various drafts and revisions are set out in Becker, *Declaration of Independence*; and Julian Boyd, *The Declaration of Independence: The Evolution of the Text as Shown in Facsimiles of Various Drafts by its Author* (Washington, DC, 1943). The history of the reputation of the document until 1826 is set out in Philip F. Detweiler, 'The Changing Reputation of the Declaration of Independence: The First Fifty Years', *William and Mary Quarterly*, 3rd series, 19 (1962).

The most important book on the philosophical underpinning of the revolution is Bernard Bailyn, *Ideological Origins of the American Revolution* (Cambridge, MA, 1967), and this work was built upon the very extensive literature which preceded it. In particular see Louis Hartz, *The Liberal Tradition in America: An Interpretation of American Liberal Thought since the Revolution* (New York, 1955). More recent revisions and qualifications to this monumental tradition can be found in Lance Banning, *The Jeffersonian Persuasion: Evolution of a Party Ideology* (Ithaca, 1978); and in two works by Joyce Appleby: *Capitalism and a New Social Order: The Republican Vision of the 1790s* (New York, 1984), and her extremely helpful collection of essays, *Liberalism and Republicanism in the Historical Imagination* (Cambridge, MA, 1992).

For an account of Jefferson's extraordinary multifaceted intelligence and its deep roots in the culture from which he came see Daniel J. Boorstin, *The Lost World of Thomas Jefferson* (Chicago, 1948, new ed, 1993) and Merrill D. Peterson, *The Jefferson Image in the American Mind* (New York, 1960).

A more recent and thoroughly readable re-creation of the relations between the most important Founding Fathers is Joseph J. Ellis, *Founding Brothers: The Revolutionary Generation* (New York, 2000); and for a slightly different emphasis Stuart Leibiger, *Founding Friendship: George Washington, James Madison and the Creation of the American Republic* (Charlottesville, 1999). Jefferson's inventions of writing technologies is the subject of Silvio Bedini, *Thomas Jefferson and his Copying Machines* (Charlottesville, 1984).

For a good overview of the political process which resulted in the creation of the United States see Merrill Jensen, *The Founding of a Nation: A History of the American Revolution, 1763–1776* (New York, 1966); and for the legal context in which the Declaration was made see John Philip Reid, 'The Irrelevance of the Declaration', in Hedrick Hartog, ed., *Law in the American Revolution and the Revolution of the Law* (New York, 1981).

For an exemplary account of the context in which the Declaration was made and the so-called 'other' declarations see the second chapter of Maier's *American Scripture*. Two books are indispensable for the strange turns in the historiography attached to the Mecklenburg declaration: William Henry Hoyt, *The Mecklenburg Declaration of Independence* (New York, 1907); and V. V. McNitt, *Chain of Error and the Mecklenburg Declarations of Independence* (Palmer, MA, 1960).

CHAPTER 2

An account of the first observance of the Fourth by legislative enactment, held at Salem, North Carolina, is to be found in *July 4th, 1783: A Day of Thanksgiving* (Winston-Salem, NC, 1966).

The fiftieth celebrations in 1826 are the subject of a recent book by Andrew Burstein, *America's Jubilee* (New York, 2001), to which my own account is indebted. The first hundred years of orations is the subject of Paul Goetsch and Gerd Hurm, eds., *The Fourth of July: Political Oratory and Literary Reactions* (Tubingen, 1992). The early chapters of Appelbaum, *The Glorious Fourth*, also cover this ground, as do Travers, *Celebrating the Fourth*, and Hay, 'Freedom's Jubilee'.

Orations are the subject of Henry A. Hawken, *Trumpets of Glory: Fourth of July Orations, 1786–1861* (Granby, CT, 1976). Earlier studies include Cedric Larsen, 'Patriotism in Carmine: 162 Years of July 4th Oratory', *Quarterly Journal of Speech*, February 1940; and Howard Martin, 'The Fourth of July Oration', *Quarterly Journal of Speech*, December 1958. For the Boston context see Gerd Hurm, 'The Rhetoric of Continuity in Early Boston Orations', in Goetsch and Hurm, *The Fourth of July*. Of the many orations published those which give a very good insight into their time include Edward Everett, *Orations and Speeches on Various Occasions* (Boston, 1856); Hugh Henry Brackenridge, 'Oration on the Celebration of the Anniversary of Independence, July 4th, 1793', in *A Hugh Henry Brackenridge Reader, 1770–1815*, ed. Daniel Marder (Pittsburgh, 1970); Daniel Webster, 'Fourth of July Oration' (1802), in *The Writings and Speeches* (Boston, 1903); and Frederick Saunders, ed., *Our National Centennial Jubilee: Orations, Addresses and Poems Delivered on the Fourth of July, 1876, in Several States of the Union* (New York, 1877).

The formula for Boston Fourth speeches is reproduced in many pamphlets of the first half of the nineteenth century. See on this James Spear Loring, *The Hundred Boston Orators Appointed by the Municipal Authorities and Other Public Bodies from 1770 to 1852* (Boston, 1853).

For the tradition of celebration established in North Carolina see Fletcher M. Green, 'Listen to the Eagle Scream: One Hundred Years of the Fourth of July in North Carolina, 1776–1876', in *Democracy in the Old South and Other Essays* (Nashville, 1969).

Toasts and other forms of address occasioned by the celebration of the Fourth have been collected in Philip S. Foner, ed., *The Democratic–Republican Societies, 1790–1800: A Documentary Sourcebook of Constitutions, Declarations, Addresses, Resolutions, and Toasts* (Westport, CT, 1976).

On the last hours of Adams and Jefferson see John E. Ferling, *John Adams: A Life* (Knoxville, 1992); David G. McCullough, *John Adams* (New York, 2001); W. S. Randall, *Thomas Jefferson: A Life* (New York, 1993); and Merrill D. Peterson, *Thomas Jefferson: A Reference Biography* (New York, 1986).

CHAPTER 3

Canby's paper can be consulted online at http://www.ush-istory.org/betsy/more/canby.htm. There are many web pages devoted to the Betsy Ross story, the most efficient means for accessing them is at http://www.ushistory.org/betsy/flagtale.html.

The most substantial account of cultural attitudes to the flag can be found in Scot Guenter, *The American Flag, 1777–1924: Cultural Shifts from Creation to Codification* (Rutherford, NJ, 1990). For more anecdotal histories see James A. Moss, *The Flag of Our United States* (Chicago, 1940); Michael Corcoran, *For Which it Stands: An Anecdotal Biography of the American Flag* (New York, 2002); and Richard H. Schneider, *Stars and Stripes Forever: The History, Stories, and Memories of Our American Flag* (New York, 2003). An outstanding illustrated catalogue of the varieties of flags produced from the birth of the republic to today is Boleslaw Mastai and Marie-Louise d'Otrange Mastai, *The Stars and Stripes: The American Flag as Art and as History from the Birth of the Republic to the Present* (New York, 1973).

For an immensely detailed and fascinating account of the controversy occasioned by the trials of Gregory Lee Johnson for desecration of the flag see Robert Justin Goldstein, *Burning the Flag: The Great 1989–1990 American Flag Desecration Controversy* (Kent, OH, 1996). For the longer history of desecration see his *Desecrating the American Flag: Key Documents of the Controversy from the Civil War to 1995* (Syracuse, NY, 1996).

The pledge of allegiance is the focus of a study by John Baer, *The Pledge of Allegiance, A Centennial History, 1892–1992* (Annapolis, MD, 1992).

The story of the Liberty Bell is told in Olga W. Hall-Quest, *The Bell that Rang for Freedom: The Liberty Bell and its Place in American History* (New York, 1965); Charles S. Keyser, *The Liberty Bell* (Philadelphia, 1893); Victor Rosewater, *The Liberty Bell: Its History and Significance* (New York, 1926); Charles Michael Boland, *Ring in the Jubilee: The Epic of America's Liberty Bell* (Riverside, CT, 1973); and David Kimball, *Venerable Relic: The Story of the Liberty Bell* (Philadelphia, 1989). The story of the building in which it was first housed can be found in Edward M. Riley, *The Story of Independence Hall* (Gettysburg, PA, 1954); and Charlene Mires, *Independence Hall in American Memory* (Philadelphia, 2002). Of the many books for young readers on the bell perhaps the most appealing is Wayne Whipple, *The Story of the Liberty Bell* (Philadelphia, 1910).

For an account of Andrew McNair, the doorkeeper to

the Pennsylvania Assembly in 1776, see Mary D. Alexander, *Andrew McNair and the Liberty Bell, 1776* (Chicago, 1929).

An early source for many of the myths surrounding the birth of the nation and its early years is George Lippard, *Legends of the American Revolution* (Philadelphia, 1847).

Material on Uncle Sam is predominantly anecdotal. The best historical account is to be found in Alton Ketchum, *Uncle Sam: The Man and the Legend* (New York, 1959); a good source of illustrative material is Elinor Lander Horwitz, *The Bird, the Banner, and Uncle Sam: Images of America in Folk and Popular Art* (Philadelphia, 1976).

CHAPTER 4

On Lincoln and Gettysburg see Gary Wills, *Lincoln at Gettysburg: The Words that Made America* (New York, 1992).

On Frederick Douglass see James A. Colaiaco, *Frederick Douglass and the Fourth of July* (New York, 2006); and Bernard W. Bell, 'The African-American Jeremiad and Frederick Douglass' Fourth of July 1852 Speech', in Goetsch and Hurm, *The Fourth of July.*

On the centennial celebrations see John S. Ingram, *The Centennial Exhibition Described and Illustrated* (Philadelphia, 1877); and John D. MacCabe, *The Illustrated History of the Centennial Exhibition* (Philadelphia, 1876).

The tradition of celebration of the Fourth in Bristol, Rhode Island, is the subject of an informative illustrated book by Richard V. Simpson, *Independence Day: How the Day is Celebrated in Bristol, Rhode Island* (Bristol, RI, 1989).

On alternative declarations see Philip S. Foner, ed., *We, the Other People* (Urbana, IL, 1976).

A good illustrated guide to important Fourth celebrations

at Monticello is *The Great Birthday of Our Republic: Celebrating Independence Day at Monticello* (Chapel Hill, NC, 2003).

For books written for children about the Fourth see the database compiled by James R. Heintze, http://gurukul.american.edu/heintze/children.htm. Those particularly useful to the current study include Alice Dalgliesh, *The Fourth of July Story* (New York, 1987); James Giblin, *Fireworks, Picnics, and Flags* (New York, 1983); Lynda Graham-Barber, *Doodle Dandy! The Complete Book of Independence Day Words* (New York, 1992); Mary Jo Borrenson, *Let's Go to the First Independence Day* (Toronto, 1962); Barbara Brenner, *If You Were There in 1776* (New York, 1994); Russell Freedman, *Give Me Liberty! The Story of the Declaration of Independence* (New York, 2000); Stan Hoig, *It's the Fourth of July* (New York, 1995); Leslie C. Kaplan, *Independence Day* (New York, 2004); David F. Marx, *Independence Day* (New York, 2001); Cass R. Sandak, *Patriotic Holidays* (New York, 1990); Tom Shachtman, *America's Birthday: The Fourth of July* (New York, 1986); and Delno C. West and Jean M. West, *Uncle Sam and Old Glory* (New York, 2000).

ILLUSTRATIONS

Endpapers: John Trumbull, *The Declaration of Independence* (Washington, Capitol Version)

PICTURE CREDITS

U. S. Capitol Historical Society: endpapers, 1

While every effort has been made to contact copyright-holders of illustrations, the author and publishers would be grateful for information about any illustrations where they have been unable to trace them, and would be glad to make amendments in further editions.

ACKNOWLEDGEMENTS

I am extremely grateful to the following who read my manuscript before it reached a final draft and gave me the benefit of their comments: Christine Adams, Mary Beard, Peter Carson, Greg Polletta and Chris Prendergast. Both Mary Beard and Peter Carson acted in their capacities as professional readers for the press. It would be difficult to imagine more congenial or supportive people with whom to work. The others named acted out of friendship. Not for the first time Greg Polletta read me with a level of attention and care that no author can ever take for granted. And, also not for the first time, I have been enabled to read my own words with a precision that would have been lacking but for his kind and judicious comments. I have also been fortunate to be able to draw on the resources of a continuous – and continuing – conversation with Chris Prendergast, author of a kind of companion to this volume on 14 July. His questions and comments have never been less than testing; often they allowed me to see what I had missed, occasionally they caused me to rethink my argument. As I wrote this book his conversation was never out of earshot; I'm sure some of the decisions I have made regarding style, emphasis and tone may still irritate him or leave him unpersuaded but I took them in the knowledge that what I have to say is unlikely to find a more astute, critical and informed reception. My first reader, Christine Adams, allowed me to open a window onto the world that lies outside the enclosure of one's writing and thought. Not for the first time I beheld what I was enabled to see with pleasure and instruction. This fourth, like one previously, is for her.

INDEX

PROFILES IN HISTORY

Love affairs, battles, discoveries and rebellions have changed the course of world history. But some have turned out to be more significant than others: they have become icons in popular imagination, in drama, fiction and art; they have been argued and puzzled over, re-told and re-presented for centuries.

The *Profiles in History* series will explore some of these iconic events and relationships of history. Each book will start from the historical moment: what happened? But each will focus too on the fascinating and often surprising after-life of the story concerned.

Profiles in History is under the general editorship of Mary Beard.

Published
David Horspool: **Why Alfred Burned the Cakes**
Ian Patterson: **Guernica**
Clare Pettitt: **Dr Livingstone, I Presume?**
James Sharpe: **Remember Remember the Fifth of November**
Greg Woolf: **Et Tu, Brute?**

Unpublished
Robert Irwin: **The Summer of '67**
Christopher Prendergast: **The Fourteenth of July**
Glyn Williams: **A Hero's Death: Captain Cook and the Judgement of History**
Clair Wills: **Dublin 1916: The Siege of the GPO**
Emily Wilson: **The Death of Socrates**